SO-ARK-520

# THE ARCHITECTURE OF
# HESIODIC POETRY

**AJP Monographs in Classical Philology**

This series of publications of the *American Journal of Philology* is intended to meet a need in the broad field of classical studies. Its primary purpose is to publish and to encourage the publication of significant work that is too long to appear in article form and too short for a conventional book (that is, manuscripts of between one hundred and two hundred pages). The series covers Greek and Roman literature, textual criticism, classical linguistics, ancient philosophy, history, and Greek and Latin epigraphy.

Series Editor: Diskin Clay

1. *Basil Lanneau Gildersleeve: An American Classicist,* edited by Ward W. Briggs, Jr., and Herbert W. Benario
2. *The Heroic Muse: Studies in the* Hippolytus *and* Hecuba *of Euripides,* by David Kovacs
3. *The Architecture of Hesiodic Poetry,* by Richard Hamilton

# THE ARCHITECTURE OF HESIODIC POETRY

**Richard Hamilton**

**THE JOHNS HOPKINS UNIVERSITY PRESS**
Baltimore and London

© 1989 The Johns Hopkins University Press
All rights reserved
Printed in the United States of America

The Johns Hopkins University Press
701 West 40th Street
Baltimore, Maryland 21211

The Johns Hopkins Press Ltd.
London
*The paper used in this publication meets the minimum requirements of American National Standard for Information Sciences—Permanence of Paper for Printed Library Materials, ANSI Z39.48-1984.* ⊗

**Library of Congress Cataloging-in-Publication Data**

The Architecture of Hesiodic poetry.

(AJP monographs in classical philology ; 3)
Bibliography: p.
Includes index.
    1. Hesiod—Technique.  2. Hesiod. Theogony.
3. Hesiod. Works and days.  4. Epic poetry, Greek—
History and criticism.  I. Hesiod.  II. Hamilton,
Richard, 1943–  .  II. Series.
PA 4012.Z5A89  1989     881'.01     88-46117
ISBN 0-8018-3819-3

*The printer's device on the cover of this book is that of Aldus Manutius. It was selected from among the ones especially created in stained glass for the Hutzler Undergraduate Reading Room on the Homewood campus of The Johns Hopkins University.*

# CONTENTS

Preface      vii

PART I. THE THEOGONY

Chapter One
INTRODUCTION TO PART I      3

Chapter Two
SCHOLARSHIP      4

Chapter Three
THE PROEM      10

Chapter Four
THE DIGRESSIONS      20

Chapter Five
SUMMING UP      41

PART II. THE WORKS AND DAYS
Chapter Six
INTRODUCTION TO PART II      47

Chapter Seven
THE PROGRAM      53

Chapter Eight
THE FORM OF THE CALENDAR      67

Chapter Nine
THE DAYS      78

Chapter Ten
CONCLUSION      85

Appendices      89

Notes      107

Bibliography      125

Index of Works and Passages      129

Index of Scholars      143

PREFACE

The following investigation of the structure of Hesiod's two extant poems,*Theogony* and *Works and Days*, concentrates on the poorly
understood parts of each poem, the digressions of the *Theogony* and
the second half of the *Works and Days*, to see how they contribute to
the form of the whole. The digressions, while recognized individually,
have never been treated as a group and the formal problems their
existence poses remain unstated and unsolved. The formal problems
of the *Works and Days*, on the other hand, have been recognized for
over a century and critics have offered different strategies for dealing
with what seems on first and second reading to be a jumbled mass of
material, but no one has offered more than a perfunctory attempt at
articulating a design for the whole even though that attempt yields,
as we will see, gratifyingly positive results.

This study focuses narrowly on the works themselves and its
target is the delicate web of echoes into which the poems are woven.
Near Eastern analogues are ignored, not because they have no light
to shed on the question of form but because the light is, given the
history of our texts, uneven. The first level of literary excavation must
be the text itself, under which, one hopes, can be found earlier structures conforming to the uppermost one. The question of oral tech-
nique is likewise passed over—first because even the *minimae partes* of
oral poetry are still moot and secondly because we know virtually
nothing about the larger structures of Greek oral hexameter poetry.
So, rather than appealing to any notion of what the shape of an oral
poem can be, it seemed more prudent to begin with the poems themselves (be they oral or not) and allow the results to become ammuni-
tion for either side in the continuing oral battle.

This study is divided into two separate parts even though the
method is the same in both: the parts were conceived separately (the
former begun in 1980) and have an integrity which seemed worth
preserving. Also, in this way the pelorophobic reader will be able to
begin with the second part and not be lost. I am grateful to the Trust-
ees of Bryn Mawr College for sabbatical leave in 1985 during which
the second part of this study was completed and to numerous col-

leagues who have tolerated various drafts of various pieces of the whole, especially Julia Haig Gaisser, Mabel Lang, Carter Philips, and Peter M. Smith. Finally the indefatigable editor of this series is to be praised for his discernment and magnanimity.

Richard Hamilton
Bryn Mawr College
23 December 1987

# Part I

# The *Theogony*

## Chapter One
## INTRODUCTION TO PART I

    Although Hesiod's *Theogony* is recognized as an invaluable document for early Greek religion, philosophy, myth and linguistics, its poetic qualities are less appreciated. This is particularly true of its form. It is often said to be filled with interpolations and its author condemned as an indifferent narrator who bends, spindles and mutilates the stories he has inherited. The following essay assumes the opposite, that the poem is a coherent artistic unity whose complexity reflects a poetics quite different from that governing the rest of extant epic—except for Hesiod's own *Works and Days*—and so we should not judge him by their standards. Whereas the Homeric poet never describes himself, except for one phrase in the Hymn to Apollo, Hesiod gives us extensive personal narratives in both *Theogony* and *Works and Days*. Whereas the Homeric poet gives a continuous narrative, Hesiod in both poems composes in juxtaposed blocks, some narrative, some not, whose contrast and balance are important organizing devices.

    The crucial fact about the form of the *Theogony*, one virtually ignored by critics, is that the poem is articulated by the outline of its content given at the end of the hymn with which it begins. Furthermore, the narrative sections that fall outside this outline are arranged in a chronological and thematic pattern that counterpoints the order of the main narrative. This pattern is completed only the "investiture" narrative of the proem which represents the poem's latest moment chronologically. As the poem moves forward, the gap established by the investiture lessens until at the end it has disappeared completely, as has the gap between the birth of the Muses and their subject. In this sense the poem ends where it began and thereby fulfills the Muses' requirement that they be sung "first and last."

Chapter Two
SCHOLARSHIP

Not even the most conservative of critics now takes the Theogony as
we have it . . . to be a unified work. It has obviously suffered major
expansions and omissions as well as many minor interpolations.[1]

Kirk's pronouncement at the Entretiens Hardt on Hesiod in 1960 met
with little rebuttal at the time although most of his "major expansions" were challenged in 1966 by West in his commentary on the
*Theogony* and by Walcot in his book *Hesiod and the Near East*.[2] It is
discouraging to realize that this debate is in many ways a re-run of
that between conservative and radical points of view of the late 19th
and early 20th centuries, as recorded by Schmid (259) in 1929:

Dass hier ein in allem Wesentlichen durchaus planmässig angelegtes
Werk vorliegt, dass die auf den ersten Anblick befremdlichen Verset-
zungen und Einkeilungen grossenteils wohl begründet sind, ist ebenso
klar, als dass es an kleineren Zusätzen und Umarbeitungen aus spä-
terer Zeit nicht fehlt. Die sinnlosen Metzeleien, die ein ebenso bes-
chränkter wie selbstbewusster Rationalismus im vorigen Jahrhundert
im Text der Theogonie anzurichten liebte, werden jetzt glücklicher-
weise nicht mehr unbedingt als Beweise methodischen Scharfsinns be-
wundert.

Moreover, to judge from the recent work by Solmsen (1982) we may
be moving once again toward Kirk's position: "the battle over the authenticity of various passages is still being joined" (Mondi 325).
    A serious problem in the unitarian position has been the appar-
ently chaotic structure of the work as a whole:

It is hard to find safe criteria for judging interpolation in an author
like Hesiod. Both his extant poems show a certain diffuseness, a tendency to be side-tracked from the matter in hand, which leads one to
doubt whether they ever possessed any logical or rigorous arrangement. (Barron 96; see also Griffin 95, Mondi 327)

As we will see, recent attempts to describe the poem's form have not
been very successful.
    First an outline. The *Theogony* begins with a prologue praising
the Muses and calling upon them to sing the race of the gods (1–115).
This leads to a description of the generation of the first gods (116–

32, including two of Night's progeny, Day and Aither) and then the children of Gaia and Ouranos (133–53) who are finally released from their mother's womb by the castration of Ouranos (154–210). We next hear of the offspring of Night (211–32) and then the children and grandchildren of Pontos (233–69), ending with a series of monstrous children belonging to Phorcys and Keto, who are killed by Perseus, Bellerophon and Heracles (270–336). The account of the grandchildren of Gaia and Ouranos which follows (337ff) includes a description of Zeus giving *timai* to Styx and her children (386–403), a "hymn" to Hecate (416–52), the narrative of Zeus's deception of Kronos (459–500) and, finally, the story of the battle of wits between Zeus and Prometheus (521–616). Next come two battles, Olympians versus Titans (617–728) and Zeus versus Typhoeus (820–80), separated by a description of Tartarus, where the defeated Titans were sent (729–819). We turn then to Zeus's offspring (886–926), offspring of other Olympians (927–37), liaisons between gods (mainly Zeus's line) and mortal women (938–62) and, after another invocation of the Muses (963–68), liaisons between goddesses and men (969–1020) and finally one further invocation of the Muses (1021f).

The most notable attempts to describe the structure of the *Theogony* in the last few decades have been those of Brown (1953), Walcot (1966), West (1966) and Thalmann (1984).[3] Walcot (xiii) defines the structure of the *Theogony* as two pairs of stories (castration of Ouranos 154–210 plus deception of Kronos 459–500 and Titanomachy 617–728 plus Typhoeus episode 820–80) each internally separated by a "non-dramatic intermezzo": the description of the offspring of Night, Pontos, Ouranos (211–458) which comes between the Ouranos and Kronos stories and the description of Tartarus (729–819) which comes between Titanomachy and Typhoeus episodes. The center of the whole pattern is the Prometheus story (521–616): "it is this arrangement of stories which holds the Theogony together and gives it its unity of structure."[4]

It is the virtue of Walcot's analysis to have treated the various parts of the poem as self-standing blocks and to have focussed our attention on the pairing of stories, but there are several problems. The castration of Ouranos and the tricking of Kronos both tell of the birth of Ouranos' offspring, which is one of the subjects of the poem as announced in 105ff, and so they can hardly be formally equated with the non-genealogical story of the Titanomachy or separated in terms of content from the genealogies of the children of Night (211–

32) and Pontos (234–336), also announced as subjects of the poem in 105ff. Furthermore, in addition to the genealogies of the children of Night and Pontos, the first "non-dramatic intermezzo" contains an extended section about Hecate and a series of stories about Heracles killing the offspring of Keto, yet Walcot lumps them all together and equates them with the more obviously unified description of Tartarus which separates the Titanomachy from the Typhoeus section. A final objection is that the proposed unity is simply formal: the balancing of pairs of stories around a central one has no meaning in itself, and Walcot is able to supply no convincing reason for the emphasis on Prometheus that his structure gives. He says that it "accounts for the origin of at least one of the two sexes" (62); yet it was the origin of man(kind) not woman that was listed as the Muses' song in v.50, and the outline of the poem in 105ff does not mention mortals at all. Walcot asserts that "a necessary supplement to the birth of the gods is the appearance on earth of their human worshippers," not realizing that the Prometheus story does not describe but merely presupposes man's appearance.[5]

Brown avoids Walcot's pitfalls of selectivity and arbitrary labelling, but his end-result is not very impressive. He divides the poem into twelve sections, in which he finds "the systematic alternation of emphasis on either the divine, the human, or the physical aspect of the cosmos" (13):[6]

    I   (1–115) Invocation of the Muses .................divine, human
   II   (116–153) Void, Earth; Sky, Mountains,
        Sea; Titans, Cyclopes, Hundred-Arms ............divine, physical
  III   (154–210) Cronus castrates Sky ...................divine
   IV   (211–336) Curses of Night, blessings
        of Nereids; marvels and monsters of Sea .........human
    V   (337–382) Rivers, Sun, Moon, Dawn, Winds,
        Stars ...........................................physical
   VI   (383–403) Zeus' alliance with Styx ...............divine
  VII   (404–452) Zeus, Hecate, and mankind ............divine, human
 VIII   (453–506) Zeus' conflict with Cronus (first
        phase)........................................... divine
   IX   (507–616) Zeus, Prometheus, and mankind .......divine, human
    X   (617–735) Zeus' conflict with Cronus (final
        phase) ..........................................divine
   XI   (736–819) Tartarus and the realm of Night .......human, physical
  XII   (881–1022) Zeus' monarchy and offspring .........divine, human.

His sections follow the traditional divisions of the poem and his labels seem reasonable for the most part although section V is concerned with human as well as physical (cf 347), section III mentions human as well as divine (197, 204) and section XI involves divine (esp.775–806). More upsetting, the supposed "systematic alternation" is not at all apparent from the chart.

Brown goes on to pair the sections:

> Sharp breaks isolate the first and last sections, while the ten intervening sections fall into five groups of pairs. Sections II and III are bound together by the anticipations of conflict between Sky and his children . . . Sections IV and V are bound together . . . by an abrupt shift from narrative to catalogue style . . . Sections VI and VII are linked together as, strictly speaking, anachronistic anticipations of Zeus' new order . . . Sections VIII-XI show discontinuity and conflict between Zeus and the older powers . . . In Section XII . . . Zeus finally resolves the problem of conflict in the divine cosmos. (13f)

This pairing, such as it is (there are in fact only three pairs), seems to be extremely artificial, depending first on theme (conflict of generations), then form (catalogues) and then function (anticipation of Zeus's reign). One wonders, finally, whether section XII is part of the pattern or isolated from it.

West's analysis of the poem is by far the most detailed. He describes the poem as a combination of genealogy and narrative: "if the Succession Myth is the backbone of the *Theogony*, the genealogies are its flesh and blood" (31). In terms of structure, however, he seems to think that the order of the poem is the order of its genealogies, in which several principles can be observed (37–39):

> (1) The order is basically chronological. Each generation is dealt with, in the surviving collateral branches, before the next is taken up.
>
> (2) If, however, the end of a branch is in sight, it is often followed to its end, instead of being deferred to the next generation.
>
> (3) Where possible, related sections are made adjacent. The effect of this is sometimes a chiasmus.
>
> (4) In other cases, families are arranged in the same order as that in which the parents were first listed. . . . But the Titans form an exception to this rule. . . . The order of these six families is determined rather by the mythological digressions which attach to four of them (Kreios-Styx, Koios-Hecate, Kronos-birth of Zeus, Iapetos-Prometheus). These four are placed last, and in ascending order of length of digression.[7]

This is a confusing arrangement. In terms of structure, the most obvious feature of the genealogies, as we will see in the following chapter, is the chiastic structure (principle #3): children of Ouranos (154–210), children and grandchildren of Night (211–32), children and grandchildren of Pontos (233–336), grandchildren of Ouranos (337–616). There are problems with the other three principles. #1 takes no account of Typhoeus, the child of Gaia and Tartarus, who, since he is of a branch collateral with that of the children of Pontos and Ouranos, should *not* come after the grandchildren of Pontos, but does (820–80). Nor does #1 explain, as does #3, why the grandchildren of Pontos precede those of Ouranos or why the great-grandchildren of Pontos (Geryon 287, Orthos 309, Cerberus 311, Hydra 313, Phix 326, Nemean Lion 327) are described so much sooner than those of Ouranos (i.e., the progeny of Zeus and other Olympians 886ff). #2 contradicts #1 explicitly and its criterion of length ("if the end is in sight") does not work for the children of Kronos (thus the need for West's "often").

The analysis of the digressions in #4 is liable first to the criticism that since the "birth of Zeus" can hardly be labelled a digression and the Styx and Hecate episodes deal with the distribution of *timai* announced in the prologue (v.112) neither should be equated with the true digression about Prometheus. Secondly, this pattern cannot be extended to include the whole work (nor does West try to extend it).[8] The digression on Tartarus, unless heavily interpolated is longer than the story of Typhoeus; the castration of Ouranos is longer than the birth of Zeus. We are left, then, with a Hesiod who composes on purely formal grounds, without regard for the surrounding material.

Thalmann's analysis is a refinement of Walcot's and is liable to the same criticisms of artificiality and arbitrary selection. He describes the poem's form as three pairs of framing episodes, arranged chiastically (ABCCBA), surrounding three "groups of passages that, though self-contained, show a progress that culminates in Zeus's victory" (40). Thus (A) the proemium (1–115) is paired with Zeus's ascent to power and his various marriages (881–?929) in that both show "the world order under Zeus" (40); (B) the birth of Gaia's first offspring and the first stage of the succession story (116–210) are paired with the birth of her last child Typhoeus, Zeus's last enemy (820–80); and (C) Night's progeny (211–32) are paired with the description of Tartarus (721–819) "by her own reappearance there with her children Sleep and Death" (39) and by the subtle echo of Eris's children

(226–32) in 782–93. So much for the framing pairs. Thalmann himself admits that there are other "strong resemblances" unaccounted for by his scheme but says dismissively that sections can function "one way in their immediate surroundings and another in the design of the poem as a whole" (39), without specifying what he means or demonstrating it. Furthermore, the pairings are not obvious and in some cases arbitrary. Thus (A) the proem has often been compared with Zeus's marriages (the birth of the Muses is, after all, recounted in both places) but never with the preceding coronation of Zeus and distribution of honors, and this scheme ignores the sections such as Tartarus and Hecate which show Zeus's world order. Also, (B) the battle with Typhoeus is hardly the last element in the succession story, as Thalmann himself admits; and (C) the 22 lines about Night and her progeny do not balance the 99 lines describing Tartarus nor are those creatures by any means the only inhabitants of Tartarus—in fact, as we will see, virtually all of the genealogies of the first part of the poem have a place there.

Within the three chiastic pairs, Thalmann finds three groups: (1) offspring of Pontos and Oceanus; (2) marriages of other Titans, ending with Styx and Hecate; (3) marriage of Rhea and Kronos; battle with Titans. Thalmann's first two "groups" within the chiastic pairs have considerable plausibility: the offspring of Pontos and the offspring of Oceanus both end with a "long list of daughters" (he might have noted that both lists are aquatic and both many times longer than any other list in the poem) while Styx and Hecate are clearly parallel in being a single female divinity benefited by Zeus's distribution of honors. The third "group," however, is not a pair like the first two and is even interrupted by the Prometheus episode. Instead of pairing the tricking of Kronos and the tricking by Prometheus, Thalmann argues that the "line of Iapetos, with the crucial Prometheus episode, is thus framed by the narrative of the struggle with the Titans" (41). In the end we return to a form of Walcot's scheme, with Prometheus in the center, even though Thalmann was critical of this.

Despite a number of good points, none of these critics has been able to show that the whole poem is carefully unified. Their main fault has been to ignore the poet's own statement about the content of the poem, the so-called 'program' contained in lines 106–115 of the proem, to which we now turn.

Chapter Three
THE PROEM

The form of the proem is quite complex. We begin with the Helikonian Muses singing and dancing on Mt. Helikon (1–21). We then hear how they once taught the shepherd Hesiod, gave him a σκῆπτρον and ordered him to sing the race of gods (γένος αἰὲν ἐόντων) singing themselves first and last (22–34). Hesiod breaks from this narration with a dismissive question (35), and we begin again with the Muses, hearing first how they sing on Olympus about the race of gods and Zeus's power (36–52), then how they were born near Olympus (53–67), how they once travelled there singing of Zeus (68–76), who they are and what benefits they confer on kings and poets (77–103). The poet then bids them farewell (104) and orders them to sing the race of gods and how they gained control of Olympus (105–15).

These stops and starts are confusing. Fortunately the poet has given his audience some clear directions. The first line of the proem announces by its form that it is a hymn of the Homeric type.[1] This does not tell us all that we need to know since such hymns vary anywhere from a few to a few hundred lines but it does at least mark the proem's beginning and end formulaically: v.1 (Μουσάων Ἑλικωνιάδων ἀρχώμεθ' ἀείδειν) is a standard beginning formula as we can see from the beginning of the *Hymn to Demeter*, Δήμητρ' ἠΰκομον σεμνὴν θεὰν ἄρχομ' ἀείδειν (see also Hymn XXII, XXVI, XXVIII) while v.104 (χαίρετε, τέκνα Διός, δότε δ' ἱμερόεσσαν ἀοιδήν) is one of the standard sign-off formulae, to which we can compare Hymn X.4–5, χαῖρε θεὰ Σαλαμῖνος ἐϋκτιμένης μεδέουσα / εἰναλίης τε Κύπρου. δὸς δ'ἱμερόεσσαν ἀοιδήν (see also VI. 19–20, XI.5, XV.9, XX.8, XXIV.5, XXVI.11–12). Hesiod complicates this simple pattern in two ways: he gives us a second 'beginning' at v.36 (τύνη, Μουσάων ἀρχώμεθα); and, after the sign-off formula, he adds a set of commands to the Muses in place of the usual promise of future song such as αὐτὰρ ἐγὼ καὶ σεῖο καὶ ἄλλης μνήσομ' ἀοιδῆς (X.6; see also II.495, III.546, IV.580, VI.21, XIX.49, XXV.7, XXVII.22, XXVIII.18, XXIX.14, XXX.19, XXXIII.19; see also V.293, IX.9, XVIII.11).

Both complications mark important changes in the Homeric format. The new beginning comes after the hymn has turned into a personal narrative of Hesiod's own confrontation with the Muses, which is given a closing formula about singing the god first and last[2] and then broken off by the poet's abrupt question: "What to me are these things concerning (or around) oak or rock" (v.35).[3] Thus the story of Hesiod's investiture appears to be somewhat at odds with its surroundings, as we might expect for a personal narrative in an impersonal Homeric form.[4] The material after the sign-off formula at v.104 transforms the Muses from objects of the song to the singers of the song, and what they are told to sing (the 'program') is in fact the poem that follows, the "theogony" proper. Thus we have not only the end of the proemial hymn in v.104 but a fixing of the actual content of the coming song, and this is confirmed by a further invocation of the Muses (ταῦτά μοι ἔσπετε Μοῦσαι 114) which we recognize as the beginning of a song from its related phrase in the first line of the *Odyssey*. This is important since several critics have recently argued that the *Theogony* as a whole is a Homeric hymn,[5] although the sign-off and second invocation should make that impossible. The only parallel for such a break-off and reinvocation is the *Hymn to Apollo* and most scholars think that this hymn is actually two hymns.[6] The *Theogony* in fact is our best evidence for the function of the Homeric hymn as proem to a longer song. Let us now consider these two complications further.

### A. The New Beginning

The one thing agreed upon by the many recent studies of the form of the proem is that there is a strong break at v.35.[7] It is often assumed that the contrast between the two parts of the proem is between a Helikonian song (1–35) and an Olympian one (36–104) and there certainly is some truth to this. The first part describes the Muses dancing on Mount Helikon during the night (ἐννύχιαι 10) while the second describes the birth of the Muses "a little from the highest peak of snowy Olympus" (62) and then their journey to Olympus (68ff) undoubtedly during the day. A fatal objection, however, is that the Muses are called "Olympian" in the first part (v.25) as well as the second.

What then is the point of the new beginning at v.36?[8] In the first place it highlights the special nature of the passage describing Hesiod's encounter with the Muses. He used to be a shepherd but the Muses converted him and handed him a σκῆπτρον so that he could sing past and future. This is important to modern critics since it is the first self-description by a poet and comes in a genre that to judge from Homeric epic resists such personal information. It is also important as a description of the nature of archaic poetry: the poet receives a "calling" and has a badge of office, a pattern followed by later Greek poets, notably Archilochus and Callimachus.[9] The fact that the Muses know how to lie, that the poet used to reside among shepherds, "mere bellies" (in contrast to the farming persona of the *Works and Days*), and that he is given a σκῆπτρον and not a ῥάβδος have all led to extensive discussion.[10] Finally, the Muses tell Hesiod to sing them first and last, and since Hesiod has begun his poem with them, we may expect him to end with them, as he does.[11] The topic the Muses assign Hesiod is the race of the gods, a song we have already heard the Muses themselves sing in vv.11–21 (γένος αἰὲν ἐόντων 33 = 21).

Despite the break at v.35, what follows seems closely allied to what went before: once again the poet begins with the Muses (Μουσάων ἀρχώμεθα 36-Μουσάων . . . ἀρχώμεθ' 1); once again they sing the past and future (τά τ' ἐσσόμενα πρό τ' ἐόντα 38 = 32); and once again the subject is the race of the gods.[12] Here, however, there is a definite order to the song. The first theogony of the Muses (11–21) is chaotic no matter how one juggles the lines, and it is probably meant to be chaotic.[13] It is a simple list; it begins with Zeus and Hera (11f) but it is the Argive Hera, a political localization which strikes a false note.[14] The list moves back in time through the children of Zeus (Athena, Apollo, Artemis, 13f) to his brother Poseidon (15) and then the generation of Ouranids (Leto, Iapetos, Kronos, 18) and finally the primeval powers (Gaia, Oceanus, Night, 20) but mixed in are the strange combination of Themis, Aphrodite, Hebe and Dione (16f) before the Ouranids and Dawn, Sun and Moon (19) after them.

The second theogony (θεῶν γένος 44) sung by the Muses (45–50) is, by contrast, clearly ordered: they are to sing from the beginning (ἐξ ἀρχῆς 45) and they sing first (πρῶτον 44) the children of Gaia and Ouranos and those who come after them (45f) and secondly (δεύτερον 47) Zeus, "father of gods and men" (47), "how he is the mightiest of gods and greatest in strength"(49) and then the race of men and Giants (50).[15] This last is not found in Hesiod's *Theogony* but the first two parts match its content quite well for in the main part of the poem (116ff) the children of Gaia and Ouranos are described first (133–210) then the grandchildren (337–616) and finally Zeus's conquest of the Titans (617–820) and consequent election as king (884f).

Between the two sets of Ouranid children are sandwiched the off-spring of Night (211–32) and Pontos (233–336), who were not mentioned in 45ff. In both cases children and grandchildren are lumped together whereas the children of Gaia and Ouranos are separated from their grandchildren, and we may see in this anomalous treatment of Ouranos' children their position as a separate item in the Muses' song. A further confirmation of the connection between the Muses' second song and the content of Hesiod's *Theogony* resides in Zeus's epithet: if Gaia and Ouranos produced the gods, Zeus can hardly be called the "father" of the gods. The epithet reflects the replacement of genealogy by politics and this is what we will find to be the case with Zeus's hegemony in the *Theogony*.

The "correction" in 44ff of the Muses' first song creates the expectation that there will be a corresponding correction of the investiture, where Hesiod is at the mercy of the abusive and potentially deceitful Muses. Such correction is accomplished in a way after the sign-off at v.104, where the content of the theogony is once again reviewed, here with even greater precision than in 44ff, and the poet now directs the Muses, without any hint of guile. As the Muses then commanded Hesiod to sing the race of the gods, so he now commands them to sing the race of the gods, using the same formulaic phrase: γένος αἰὲν ἐόντων (105 = 33). Furthermore, the content of the song he specifies is to be almost the same as their earlier song, with the addition of Night and Pontos: again they are to sing the children of Gaia and Ouranos (οἳ Γῆς ἐξεγένοντο καὶ Οὐρανοῦ ἀστερόεντος 106 ~ οὓς Γαῖα καὶ Οὐρανὸς εὐρὺς ἔτικτεν 45) and then their children (οἵ τ' ἐκ τῶν ἐγένοντο θεοὶ δωτῆρες ἐάων 111 = 46) and they are to sing this, once again, from the beginning (ἐξ ἀρχῆς 115 = 45). The second part of their former song, the praise of Zeus "how he is mightiest and greatest in strength" (49) is now defined as "how they divided their wealth and distributed their *timai* and how they first got Olympus with its many folds" (112f).[16] Since Zeus is the leader in the conquest of Olympus and is the one who distributes *timai*, the equation of the two songs is complete.[17]

Although this second "correction" occurs only after the hymn to the Muses has ended, it is anticipated within the hymn in two ways. First there is a subtle equation of poet and Muses in the description of the Muses' trip to Olympus to their father who "rules in heaven and has thunder and lightning, having conquered in strength his father Kronos; he distributed well each thing for the gods alike and devised *timai*" (71ff). This sounds very like the second theme of both 44ff and 105ff. The Muses are singing, and Zeus is described in terms appropriate to either past or present song. There is no clear connection at first, but at v.75 we are told to our surprise that the description of Zeus *was* their song.[18] That is, what appeared to be part of Hesiod's present song was in fact the past song of the Muses. Of course there is no essential difference and this grammatical subterfuge marks the identity of the Muses' song in 44ff and the one Hesiod commands them to sing in 105ff.

The second preparation for 105ff occurs in the long description of the Muses' relationship to kings and poets. Singers are given pride of place, just before the sign-off, and what is said recapitulates the main points of the investiture: "singers come from the Muses" (94f) and the songs which poets sing to delight men are the tales of men and "the blessed gods who hold Olympus" (101). Delight has replaced deceit and the focus is now not on the Muses but on the performance of the poet. The transition to the poet invoking the Muses to sing the race of the gods could not be made easier.

The new beginning, then, separates a song of the race of gods which is disorderly and poorly articulated and no more than a list from two later songs which are clearly defined and have narrative content, first the two-part song in 44ff and then the song about Zeus in 71ff. These songs are picked up after the sign-off of v.104 in Hesiod's own charge to the Muses, which at the same time inverts and thereby replaces the Muses' earlier charge to Hesiod. The transition is smoothed first by the implicit equation of poet and Muses as performers of the song of 71ff and by final focus on the poet as descendant of the Muses and the delight his songs about men and gods bring. A further effect of the new beginning is to mark the narrative of Hesiod's investiture as irrelevant. The point of this will become apparent once we have seen how the poem's other narratives are related. The main function of the break and new beginning, however, is to emphasize and validate the poet's charge to the Muses, the "program" of the poem.

### B. The Program

The song Hesiod asks the Muses to sing in 105ff specifies three major topics: (1) the children of Gaia and Ouranos, Night and Pontos

(106f); (2) their children (111); (3) how they divided wealth and *timai* and first got Olympus (112f). Critics continue to argue about whether there are interpolated lines here but, aside from 108–10 which add nothing essential,[19] the passage is guaranteed not only by its parallelism with the previous song of the Muses but by the rest of the poem, for it follows this program in detail. We begin with the children of Gaia and Ouranos (133–210), the children and grandchildren of Night (211–232), the children and grandchildren of Pontos (233–336) and finally the grandchildren of Gaia and Ouranos (337–616).[20] This ends the first part, the genealogical part, of the poem and the ending is marked by a return to the beginning (Gaia and Ouranos). The second part is primarily an historical account of the defeat of Kronos and the Titans, their being sent to Tartarus (617–820), Zeus' defeat of Typhoeus (820–880), the election of Zeus as king (881–85), followed by a list Zeus' progeny (886–926) and other divine progeny (927–1020). This split between the genealogical first part and the historical second part is worth stressing since critics continue to see the whole poem as genealogical:

> die Theogonie ist ein durch ein Proomion eingeleiteter Grosskatalog, dessen Anordnung im Prinzip durch die Stammbäume gegeben ist.[21]

The program raises one obvious problem. The poem proper clearly begins at 116; the question is where it ends, for it does not stop with the capture of Olympus at 885 but goes on to describe the children of Zeus (886–926) and other gods (927–62) and, after another farewell and invocation (963–68), gives further liaisons (969–1020) and a final invocation (1021f). The line just before the second command to the Muses to sing (964) seems an obvious choice as the end point. The justification for this is first the reinvocation itself, which gives a program different from that before: the Muses are now asked to sing the liaisons of goddesses and mortal men (965–68). Also, Pausanias (1.3.1) understood 986ff to be from a different work, Hesiod's *Catalogue of Women*,[22] and we should note that the third invocation of the Muses in 1021f, which forms the end of the *Theogony* in the medieval manuscripts, is shown by a papyrus to have been the beginning of the *Catalogue*: "the proem of the *Catalogue* ... was clearly designed from the start as a *re*-invocation" (West 48f).[23] That is, the end of the *Theogony* seems infinitely extensible via such reinvocations and so it seems reasonable to view the first such reinvocation as the first extension. Furthermore, the content of 969ff. seems to be for the most part elaboration. 969–74 describes the birth of Ploutos, Demeter's child by a mortal, and so continues the description of Demeter's child by Zeus, Persephone (912–14). The account of the children of Cadmus and Harmonia (975–78), belongs with 937, the marriage of Cadmus and Harmonia, while the marriage of Jason and Medea (992–1002) continues from the birth of Medea in 961f.[24] From 1003 on we hear of the great heroes, Achilles, Aeneas and Odysseus. The only parts that are not obviously extensions are the description of Geryon (979–83), which is a doublet of 287–90, and the list of Eos' children (984–91), inserted perhaps to match the earlier insertion of Helios (956–62). Understandably, most modern critics would ascribe only the part before 965 to Hesiod and many would give him much less (see appendix 3).

The listing of the children and grandchildren of Zeus (886–916), while not demanded by the program, has seemed to most critics to be an integral part of it. "The union of Zeus with an older power . . . issues in the birth of goddesses representative of a new order and harmony." So Solmsen (43), who points to the Horai as Hesiod's invention (34) and notes that Eunomie is Zeus's answer to Night's child Dysnomie (35).[25] In addition the passage continues and resolves the series of succession stories that have punctuated the genealogies. Ouranos would not let Gaia give birth to their children and so she plotted with her youngest child Kronos, who castrated Ouranos but was then burdened with the threat of vengeance (210; cf. the birth of Erinyes 185). Kronos, told that his son will defeat him, swallowed his children, but Rhea, with the help of Gaia and Ouranos, tricked Kronos "in order that he pay back the Erinys of both his father and his children" (472f) and thus Kronos too was eventually defeated by his son Zeus. Zeus in turn is faced with the same threat of producing a child who would be "king of gods and men" (897) and so swallows his future destroyer, along with its mother Metis, as did Kronos, but he is the trickster not the tricked and he does ultimately allow the birth of one of the children, unlike either Kronos or Ouranos. This appears to solve the succession problem, and the subsequent list of children seems to confirm this for it is a list primarily of Zeus's progeny, presented in a formally regular fashion.[26] In contrast to the earlier pairing of the Titans, Zeus alone mates with his sisters and he mates with all of them, except the virgin Hestia, as well as with a number of Titans (Mnemosyne, Themis) and others of the earlier generation (Leto, Metis, Eurynome) and of the later generation (Semele, Alcmene). In contrast to Zeus's far-ranging potency, we find among the male Olympians a single child of Poseidon and the childless marriage of Hades and Persephone, in which the bride was Zeus's child given by him in marriage (ἔδωκε 914), apparently voluntarily. Generation has meant the threat of succession, and by controlling generation, Zeus keeps his power.[27]

Similarly the next generation is primarily a demonstration of Zeus's control. The catalogue (933b–962) concentrates on two of his children, Dionysus and Heracles, both by mortal mothers and both granted immortality. Thus we hear first of the birth of Harmonia (along with her brothers Fear and Terror) from Zeus's child Ares and her marriage to Kadmos, which produced Semele, the mother of Dionysus by Zeus. Then we hear of the birth of Heracles, the marriage of Dionysus and Ariadne, resulting in her immortality, and finally the marriage of Heracles and Hebe and his immortality.[28] One should note that all these unions of Zeus's children are childless—marriage has replaced generation.[29]

Zeus still faces the threat of succession by a child greater than himself, one who will become "king of gods and men" in his place (897). Scholars seem to assume that the child is Athena and that Zeus has turned aside the threat by swallowing Metis, just as Kronos swallowed his dangerous child.[30] Zeus's "parthenogenic" birth of Athena through his head (symbol of wisdom, appropriate to the child of Metis) is supposed to have caused her to side with rather than against her father. The text, however, will not support this:

> for it was fated that exceedingly wise children be born from her, first the maid owl-eyed Tritogeneia, with might and thoughtful counsel equal to her father and then (αὐτὰρ ἔπειτ' 897) he was going to bear a son king of gods and men with an excessively violent heart (894–98).

Clearly there are two children who will be born, and the dangerous son will be born after Athena and so potential danger remains: "if the swallowing did not prevent the birth of Athena, it ought not to have prevented the birth of the son" (West 401).[31]

Also, Zeus faces rebellion of a sort from Hera, who matches his birth of Athena with her own parthenogenic birth of Hephaestus (927–29). In Homer Hephaestus is said to have taken part in a revolt against Zeus, led by Hera, Athena and Poseidon (*Iliad* 1.400) and it may be no accident that in the *Theogony* the only children by Olympians other than Zeus are by Poseidon and Hera. Hesiod spells out the danger from Hera by noting first that she returns us to the earlier age of birth without sex (οὐ φιλότητι μιγεῖσα 927 ~ ἄτερ φιλότητος ἐφιμέρου 132) and by mentioning that she competes against Zeus.[32] The verb used (ἐρίζω) recalls Prometheus' contest against Zeus (534) and especially the Titanomachy (637,705,710). Finally, an early Greek tradition tells us that Typhoeus was Hera's child, born after Hephaestus. We first find this in the *Hymn to Apollo* (307ff) and in Stesichorus (fr.239 PMG), but this tradition may be much older and it is conceivable that Hesiod transferred Typhoeus' parentage to Gaia from Hera.[33]

Thematically, as has long been recognized, the epilogue is the ultimate example of the poem's focus on Zeus. Zeus headed the list of the first theogony in the proem (11), was the second topic of the second (46ff), and the sole topic of the third (71–74). The description of Ouranos' children presupposes the victory of Zeus in the description of the Cyclopes as "(those) who gave thunder to Zeus and made lightning (for him)" (141). We hear about Zeus's dispensation of *timai* first with Styx and her children and then with Hecate, "for the son of Kronos did not in any way do her violence or take away the honor she had been alloted among the Titans, the earlier gods" (423f). All this is told before Zeus is even born. At his birth he is described as the "father of gods and men" (457), an Homeric phrase echoed from the proem, where it was part of the Muses' hymn of his power (47). When Kronos heard that it was fated that he be subdued by his child, he swallowed all his children, but when Zeus was born his mother substituted a rock. Zeus grew up, apparently tricked his father (494) and then forced him to disgorge the rock (and the children), which was then set up at Delphi (and may be the rock described in the proem at v.35). Zeus also released the Cyclopes and thereby gained control of lightning and thunder, "trusting in which he rules gods and men" (506). Almost the same phrasing was part of the Muses' third song in the proem:

ὁ δ᾽ οὐρανῷ ἐμβασιλεύει
αὐτὸς ἔχων βροντὴν ἠδ᾽ αἰθαλόεντα κεραυνόν
κάρτει νικήσας πατέρα Κρόνον (71–73)

The stage is now set for the Titanomachy, but the Prometheus story intrudes, in which the traditional story is blatantly manipulated to praise Zeus, despite the fact that he was duped by Prometheus. The Titanomachy itself is similarly manipulated so that Zeus plays a cen-

tral role, despite the fact that his actual effect in the battle is minimal.[34]

The epilogue, then, from 901 to 964 is rightly accepted by critics
as a natural extension of what precedes. It also forms an attractive
conclusion in its combining of genealogy and politics. At the same
time we should recognize that it contains some unresolved tensions,
that the succession story is not complete and that chronologically we
have not reached the latest point in the poem. In fact succession story
and chronological continuation of the epilogue are both found in the
three non-succession narratives that are properly termed narrative
disgressions.

## Chapter Four
## THE DIGRESSIONS

The program of 105ff leads us to expect discussion first of the children and grandchildren of Gaia, Ouranos, Night and Pontos and then description of how they took Olympus and divided their *timai*. We have already seen that that the poem continues beyond the division of *timai*; before that we find a number of other digressions. Six stand out: the fate of Keto's brood (270–336), the description of Zeus's honors to Styx and her children (386–403), the 'hymn' to Hecate (416–52), the Prometheus story (521–616), the description of Tartarus (736–819) and the Typhoeus episode (820–80).

### A. The Non-Narrative Digressions

The three non-narrative digressions all, more or less explicitly, involve Zeus's distribution of *timai* and can all be seen as Hesiod's attempt to divert his audience from and replace the usual version of the distribution. As it stands the distribution of *timai* is hardly mentioned. Only after the unexpected Typhoeus episode do we hear in the briefest possible way that the gods urged Zeus to rule and "he well divided the *timai* among them" (884f). Having been told the topic of the distribution of *timai* (112), an archaic audience would probably expect to hear of the division of the world between Zeus, Poseidon and Hades, familiar to us from *Iliad* 15.187ff:

> It was a traditional motif, but [Hesiod] did not elaborate it, because it was difficult to reconcile with his own conception of Zeus as the supreme god.[1]

What Hesiod does instead is to give us a description of the distribution of *timai* to Styx's children (386–403) and then to Hecate (412–52), while implicitly contrasting the more advanced δασμός of his account with the λάχος of the usual account.[2] We hear that Zeus gathered the Olympians and promised that anyone who helped him fight against the Titans would keep the honor (τιμήν) he had before and whoever was unhonored by Kronos would receive the appropriate honor (392–96). Hecate is an example of the former and Styx of the latter.

Styx and her children came to Zeus's side "through the plans of the father" (διὰ μήδεα πατρός 398) and were given appropriate honors, she to be the great oath of the gods and her children to sit beside him forever. Since their names are Competition (Ζῆλος), Victory (Νίκη), Power (Κράτος) and Force (Βίη), this is a thinly disguised allegory of Zeus's permanent hegemony, and so is an exact equivalent of the later election of Zeus to kingship. Hesiod signals this by ending the section, "thus he did what he promised and he himself has power (κρατεῖ) and rules" (403), clearly pointing to one of the children, Kratos. Soon thereafter Zeus uses βίη against defeated (νικηθείς) Kronos (496) and the Titans (689) and it is κράτος that finally turns the battle in the Titanomachy (710).

The value of the Hesiodic version of the distribution as opposed to the Homeric one is that Zeus has total control rather than sharing his power with his two brothers. In fact it is probably Zeus's thoughts that are being described in 398 as μήδεα πατρός. This is usually taken to refer to Styx's biological father Oceanus although he elsewhere plays no part in advising anyone, but it probably refers to her spiritual father Zeus, who has just given her advice (392–96).[3] πατήρ in the *Theogony* is used almost exclusively of Ouranos or Zeus and often of Zeus in a non-biological sense, as we have seen with θεῶν πατὴρ ἠδὲ καὶ ἀνδρῶν (47, 457, 468 cf. 542, 643, 838).[4]

The other distribution story involves Hecate, who has a share of earth, sea and heaven (413f; 427) for when men sacrifice they call on her, kings, warriors, horsemen, athletes, fishermen, and herdsmen. The two stories have similar features. As with Styx, we find glorification of νίκη, κράτος and βίη, which are even joined in one line (437). Griffith (52) argues that Hecate's three-fold power "may perhaps remind us of the threefold division by Zeus and his brothers."[5] Finally we have the same, though less obvious, focus on Zeus. Zeus was the one who allowed Hecate to keep her power. Hesiod even seems to endow Hecate with Zeus's characteristics, to judge from the prologue to the *Works and Days*. There we find Zeus described with the same repetitive, incantatory phrasing and even some of the same words: v.443 ῥεῖα δ' ἀφείλετο φαινομένην and v.447, ἐξ ὀλίγων βριάει κἀκ' πολλῶν μείονα θῆκεν closely resemble WD 6–7:

ῥέα μὲν γὰρ βριάει, ῥέα δὲ βριάοντα χαλέπτει
ῥεῖα δ' ἀρίζηλον μινύθει καὶ ἄδηλον ἀέξει.[6]

In saying that everything is done through (διά) Zeus, Hesiod puns on his name:

δεῦτε Δι'. . . /
ὅν τε διὰ . . . / (WD 2f)

and then repeats the idea in v.4, Διὸς μεγάλοιο ἕκητι. Given Hesiod's love of puns,[7] it is not absurd to imagine that he connected Hecate ('Εκάτη) too with causality (ἕκητι), specifically the causality of Zeus.[8] Some support for this is the poet's phrasing in 529 to describe Heracles' release of Prometheus, οὐκ ἀέκητι Ζηνὸς 'Ολυμπίου ὕψι μέδοντος.[9] If the connection indeed exists, Zeus is much more present than at first appears, and we might explain Hecate's universal power, which strikes us as so odd, as a result of his presence.[10]

Finally, in terms of the programmatic goals of the gods' distribution of their *timai* and their possession of Olympus (112f), the Tartarus episode (736–819) subtly presents us with a fundamental realignment analogous to the new sexual politics introduced by Zeus in the epilogue. In the epilogue the new order is, as we will see, symbolized by (1) Zeus's control of the means of production; (2) the regularity of that production; (3) the symbolic recasting of the birth of the Moirai. Generation means succession and so Zeus both controls generation in the epilogue and replaces it in the Tartarus episode with a geographical definition of individuals who before were talked of as parents and children. Just as the *timai* of Styx's children are described geographically and the μοῖρα distributed to Ajax (520) is at the ends of the earth and the perjured gods are deprived of their share (ἀπαμείρεται 801) by being excluded from the assembly of the gods, so the beings of the previous generations now become geographical locations.[11]

> Relationships which elsewhere in the *Theogony* are set forth in genealogical terms are here restated with much greater emphasis on the cosmological point of view.[12]

Strikingly, the order of the Tartarus digression is approximately that of the genealogies. Leaving aside the two structural repetitions (807ff, 811ff) which serve to delimit the digression, we find four sections of Tartarus, each introduced by an ἔνθα clause, describing first (a) the sources of earth, Tartarus, sea and heaven, and the "great gap" (736ff), then, (b) after the house shared by Night and Day (745ff), the houses of Sleep and Death (758ff), then (c) the house of Hades, guarded by Cerberus (767ff), and finally (d) the dwelling of Styx, whose oath is described in detail (775ff). This is the same order in which these beings were presented in their genealogical aspect earlier in the work: (a) Earth 117, Tartarus 119, Pontos 132, Ouranos 127, Chaos 116; (b) Sleep and Death 211f, after Night and Day 123f; then (c) Cerberus, dog of Hades 311; and finally (d) Styx 361.[13]

## B. The Narrative Digressions

We have in the core of the poem (116–885) three narrative digressions that do not involve the succession story: the fate of Keto's brood, the Prometheus story and the Typhoeus episode. Each of these is further distinguished from the succession narratives by being chronologically and genealogically anomalous.

The Typhoeus episode, which is redundant with the Titanomachy (and often excised for that reason), is also out of place chronologically and genealogically.[14] The episode is not only unpredicted by the program but ignored by its surroundings: we return after the battle with Typhoeus to the end of the Titanomachy which preceded it (881 = 820).[15] The chronology of the Typhoeus episode is indicated by its beginning "when Zeus had driven the Titans from heaven" (820), which shows that it must occur after Zeus has taken control and divided the timai (881–85). Its Hittite parallel in the Tale of Ullikummi obviously occurs after the Storm god is firmly established in power. Therefore one cannot argue that this is part of the "Succession Myth" (as does West). Nor should one follow Schwabl saying that the presence of a birth (here the winds that are bad for man) makes the episode part of the main narrative.[16] In addition to chronological displacement and absence from the program, the Typhoeus episode is anomalous in suddenly bringing us back to the aboriginal times of Gaia's mating—the last time she did this was back with the Ouranids, Cyclopes and Hundred-handers (126–53)—and here she mates with what has hitherto been treated as a place, much to the consternation of critics. The most one can say is that the Typhoeus episode shows how Zeus kept supreme power, but one must admit that critics who complain that it simply duplicates the Titanomachy seem to have a point.

Likewise, the Prometheus story is chronologically out of place: the birth of Zeus has not yet taken place, nor that of Athena and Hephaestus, all of whom are essential to the story. We return at the end to the preparation for the Titanomachy we had at the beginning—the release of the Hundred-handers (617ff) echoes that of the

Cyclopes (501ff), fleshing out the story implicit in their release and repayment. In terms of genealogy critics have noted that as we begin with the births of Atlas, Menoitios, Prometheus and Epimetheus and then hear the fates of Epimetheus, Menoitios and Atlas, we have closed the ring, outside of which stands Prometheus' story.[17] Also, critics have noted that we expect the family of Iapetos before that of Kronos not after it since Kronos was marked as the "last" child (137).[18] In terms of the program, the release of the Cyclopes which precedes the Prometheus story belongs to the Titanomachy and so we should be beyond the genealogical part of the poem.

The catalogue of the children of Phorcys and Keto is not the narrative unit that the other two non-succession narratives are but rather a series of brief stories about deaths of various progeny. The catalogue ends with offspring from the third generation in four cases being killed by Heracles (see appendix 1) so that, although none of the parts stands apart from the others in form, the whole section is peculiar in its elaboration. Moreover, the whole group is genealogically anomalous since the children are not immortal and therefore stand outside the poet's command to sing the birth of the immortal gods (105). The decapitation of Medusa, for example, resembles the castration of Ouranos in producing offspring, but the difference is that Medusa dies while Ouranos does not. In terms of chronology, the presence of Heracles and Perseus shows that we are at a point even later than with the Prometheus episode, where men were first separated from the gods. Because of the chronological gap, Hera "rears" the monsters (314, 328) rather than bearing them,[19] while the reference to the gods' "apportioning" of Echidna's location sounds as if it is later than the Olympians' apportionment after the Titanomachy.

A further similarity between the three non-succession narratives is that each contains references to mankind (Keto's brood: 329, 330; Prometheus: 535, 552, 556, 564, 569, 570, 589, 592, 600; Typhoeus: 871, 877, 879) while none of the succession narratives has any equivalent reference.[20] It is most obviously its interest in mankind that differentiates the Typhoeus episode from the Titanomachy.

An even more important similarity between the three non-succession narratives is that each seems to be paired with the immediately preceding succession narrative. Thus each of the succession narratives demanded by the program has a digressive counterpart. This pairing is clearest with Typhoeus and the Titanomachy. In fact, the close similarity of the two has been the major argument against the authenticity of the Typhoeus episode. In both stories Zeus struggles against his enemy in a contest for supreme power; in both there is a cosmic battle in which Zeus's use of thunder and lightning is decisive; in both the loser is sent to Tartarus. The parallelism includes phrasing and even structure, as West (383) following Meyer, has well demonstrated.

The Kronos-Prometheus parallelism is equally obvious, though less often noted, no doubt because the stories of Ouranos and Metis are somewhat similar.[21] In both stories we have Zeus fighting a king: Kronos is a βασιλεύς (476) and Prometheus an ἄναξ (543). In both there is a battle of wits and Zeus uses both trickery and force. This is clearer with Prometheus with the trickery of "Pandora" (δόλυν αἰπύν 589) and the binding of Prometheus and his torture by the eagle (521ff) but is also at least alluded to in 496 where Kronos relinquishes his children "conquered by the craft and strength (τέχνῃσι βίηφί τε 496) of his son." Solmsen, following Heyne, brackets 496 because it seems to conflate two means of victory (craft, violence) and, given Gaia's trickery in 494, two protagonists. Yet all royal protagonists depend to an extent on Gaia (Kronos in castrating Ouranos and learning that he was fated to be overthrown; Zeus in being saved by Gaia's advice to Rhea and then in being appointed king by her urging and finally in being told by her of his fated defeat by his son) while the double means is echoed in the Prometheus story (and implicitly in the Ouranos story). West argues (302) that Gaia's counsel in 494 refers "to the advice given to Rhea" about Zeus's fated overthrow of Kronos (475) while the τέχναι of 496 "must have been used in inducing Kronos to bring up his children."[22] This still leaves βίηφι unaccounted for since, as West himself notes, "Zeus' use of strength to overcome his father is mentioned in 73 and 490." It is more natural to interpret the βίη in 496 as the strength used by Zeus in defeating Kronos, presumably in some sort of battle.[23]

A further parallelism between Kronos and Prometheus stories is that in both there is a trick involving concealment and the voluntary taking of a deceptively wrapped object (the rock, the bones, Woman) and in both there is concealment in a belly.[24] Finally there is the odd verbal parallelism of πίονα δημῷ (referring to the fat enclosing the bones, 538) and πίονα δῆμον (referring to Zeus's hiding place, 477). The first succession story, the castration of Ouranos, is quite different: it is not a matter of wits; he is not a king; there is no belly, no trickery, no deceptive wrapping (though Kronos' concealment is implicitly deceptive).

The first set of parallel stories, the castration of Ouranos and the killing of Keto's brood, is the least complete, but has at least one striking element: in both cases a destructive cutting (castration of Ouranos, decapitation of Medusa) produces a new "child" (Aphrodite, Pegasus) who has a name which Hesiod etymologizes (Aphrodite = born in foam, ἀφρῷ 197; Pegasus = born beside streams, πηγάς 282).[25] A final link, though Hesiod has not spelled it out, is the parallelism of weapon: Kronos' δρέπανον is undoubtedly the ancestor of Perseus' falchion.

In addition to being paired with each of the main succession narratives, the non-succession narratives embody a remarkably coherent development of the end of the *Theogony*, the epilogue, in which Zeus was firmly but not fully established in power. Also we begin to see a consideration of the relation of gods and men. Although this relationship was not specified as part of the program in lines 105–115, it seems implicit in the phrase δωτῆρες ἐάων used repeatedly and solely to describe the Olympians,[26] and in Zeus's epithets, "father of gods and men" and "king of gods and men." Each of the digressive narratives shows the absolute power of Zeus, but this changes in several ways as we move further and further from the end: (a) the threat of a successor to Zeus decreases and the battles become less crucial; (b) Zeus plays an increasingly less direct role in the confrontation and depends more on subordinates first gods then men; (c) involvement with and concern for men increases. A simple diagram may make this clearer:

Ouranos castrated → Kronos defeated → Titanomachy →      epilogue
← Keto's brood ← Prometheus ← Typhoeus ←

## Typhoeus

Chronologically the Typhoeus episode is marked as later than the Titanomachy by its opening lines (820f): "When Zeus had driven the Titans from heaven, Gaia produced her youngest child, Typhoeus." Also the noise of his battle with Zeus is said to terrify Hades and the Titans (850–52); that is, the Titans are now in Hades whereas earlier the noise of the Titanomachy was said simply to reach to murky Tartarus (682).[27] There is also a progression in Zeus' ability to handle insurrection. Zeus now acts alone whereas before he had to rely on Gaia for advice,[28] the Cyclopes for his weapons and the Hundred-handers for additional support. The battle is explosive, more so than the Titanomachy, but it takes no time compared to the ten years of the previous confrontation (629–36 emphasize the duration).

Typhoeus, like Zeus's unborn child, represents a threat to Zeus's rule, as 837 makes clear: Typhoeus "would have been king of men and gods" (cf 892f). He is even called ἄναξ (859). In the *Hymn to Apollo* (307ff) Typhoeus was said to have been produced by Hera because she was angry with Zeus for bearing Athena, precisely the reason she bore Hephaestus in the *Theogony*, and we may posit a close connection between the two.[29] There are a number of hints of this in the *Theogony*. First there is the mention of Hephaestus in the simile describing Typhoeus's defeat: the monster is destroyed by a fire that is likened to the Ἡφαίστου παλάμῃσιν 866 just as later in the *Prometheus Bound* (366ff) he provides the power for Hephaestus' forge. More suggestive is the way Typhoeus "fell crippled" (ἤριπε γυιωθείς 858) after being defeated, for this resembles Hesphaestus' fall onto Lemnos after trying to help Hera overthrow Zeus, as described in *Iliad* 1.593. γυιωθείς is particularly evocative: the verb is rarely found and suggests the standard epithet of Hephaestus, ᾽Αμφιγυήεις which we find used in the *Theogony* even without the god's name (571, 579).[30] So, we move from the dangerous Hephaestus of the epilogue to the Hephaestus-like fire opposing Zeus's enemy, who now takes over Hephaestus' punishment. Hephaestus has become an ally of Zeus not his adversary, although only in a simile, and his fate has been attached to another, lesser enemy.

There is no doubt that Typhoeus represents a lesser threat than the children of the epilogue. In the first place Typhoeus is definitively defeated whereas the threat of the epilogue is not resolved. More important, the child of Zeus was *fated* to overthrow him (894), whereas it is stated that Typhoeus would have ruled only "if Zeus had not perceived sharply" (837f).[31]

Another indication of the diminution of the threat is in the simile describing Typhoeus' downfall. The Titanomachy was likened to the collapse of Heaven and Earth (702ff), and in a sense *was* the collapse of Heaven and Earth since grammatically there was no way to tell where simile began and fact ended:

> It is not clear whether Hesiod is presenting the collapse of heaven
> upon earth as something which once took place, or only as something
> that could be imagined to take place. (West 353)

If the Titans had won, Hesiod seems to be saying, we would have been
back at the beginning, when Ouranos covered Earth and would not
allow her children to be born. The simile describing Typhoeus, on
the other hand, equates the defeat of Typhoeus with the recognizable,
civilized activity of smelting:

> The flame rushed from the king hit by lightning, struck in the glens of
> the dark, rugged mountain and much of monstrous earth burned at
> the marvelous blast and melted tin-like (κασσίτερος ὥς 862) heated
> from workers' craft in the well-bored crucibles (χοάνοισι 863), or iron
> which is the strongest, tamed in the glens of the mountain by magical
> fire melts in the holy earth under Hephaestus' hands. So then earth
> melted in the gleam of the flaming fire. (859–67)

This simile, too, has unclear boundaries: the melting of earth seems
to take place in a gigantic forge.[32] Both the melting of earth and melting of metals in the forge take place "in the glens of the mountain"
(οὔρεος ἐν βήσσῃσιν 860 = 865). Secondly, the simile-marker "as" (ὥς
862) by being placed after "tin" should limit the simile to that one
word: "postpositive ὥς cannot govern a verb" (West 394). In this case
the smelting of iron "tamed by the fire" would be the actual product
of Typhoeus' burning. The masculine participle in 864 (θαλφθείς,
"heated") puts us back on track but we are still left with "in the glens
of the mountain" echoing the earlier description of Typhoeus and
blurring the line between tenor and vehicle. The similar blurring we
found in the description of the Muses' song in the prologue (68ff)
and in the Titanomachy simile marked a real equation: the Muses'
song was Hesiod's; the Titans' victory would have meant a return to
the original oppression of Gaia by Ouranos. Here the equation marks
the defeat of Typhoeus as a normal (civilized!) phenomenon, marvelous perhaps but not cataclysmic like the Titanomachy. Earth is simply
a place now—Typhoeus was her last child—and Tartarus too is
simply a place: the will have no further progeny (and should not have
had this one).[33] A final difference between the Titanomachy and the
Typhoeus episode expressed in the similes is the reference to the
present, to modern man, which is virtually absent from the programmatic portion of the poem. This difference is confirmed when we
hear that from Typhoeus come the winds harmful to man. The poet

goes on at remarkable length about the harm these winds cause both on sea and on land (872–80).

### Keto's Monstrous Brood

More important for our purpose, the kind of danger Typhoeus represents by being a snaky fiery monster appears in only one other place in the *Theogony*, also in a digressive narrative, and there the dangers are quelled not by Zeus but by his son from a mortal woman, Heracles, himself assisted by another mortal, Iolaus, and by the βου-λαί of Athena, the immortal child of Zeus. The comparison is strengthened by a number of distinctive verbal parallels. Both ὄφις (299, 322, 334, 825) and δράκων (322, 323, 825), are used only of Typhoeus and Keto's brood as is fire as an attribute (319, 324, 827, 828, surely with some Hephaestean overtones) and the word πέλωρον (295,845). ἀμήχανον is used in only these two places (295,310,836) and of Pandora (589). Only Typhoeus and Keto's brood have multiple parts of the body except for the Hundred-handers.[34] The connection between Zeus's struggle against the snaky fiery monster and Heracles' struggles against snaky monsters is reinforced by mention here of Pegasus' otherwise unattested role as purveyor of Zeus's thunder and lightning (286), the weapons he used against Typhoeus.[35] The connection is explicit in that a child of Phorcys and Keto, Echidna, actually mates with Typhaon (306).[36]

Thus the first digressive narrative and the third are paired in their descriptions of the divine adversary, but we can see a radical difference in the divine hero—in the Typhoeus episode it is Zeus acting alone in all his power and glory; here it is Zeus's son Heracles, part mortal, acting not alone but with the help of both Athena and another mortal like himself.

Another indication of the development in Zeus' methods is the reference to the βουλαί of Athena in 318. The clearest characteristic of Zeus's rule both before and after the Titanomachy is his ability to fuse thought and action, words and deeds. Kronos depended upon Gaia's advice, in fact was simply the enforcer of her plan. Zeus too is saved by Gaia's advice to Rhea and himself benefits from her advice not only in releasing the Hundred-handers and thereby winning the war, but later in swallowing Metis. He is not, however, so dependent as the others. Whereas Kronos is persuaded by Gaia, Zeus persuades the Hundred-handers; whereas Ouranos and Kronos use brute force to suppress their children, Zeus uses trickery (889) and coaxing words (890). His complete control at this point is marked by his upsetting what was fated (894) and immediately thereafter producing the Fates (904). The word that describes Zeus's fusion of thought and action is βουλή which seems in *Theogony* to mean not "counsel" as much as "decree."[37] The word is confined for the most part to Zeus himself (465,534,572,653,730) except when the Hundred-handers match Zeus's will (661, cf 653)[38] and except for two references to Athena. In 896 she is said to have βουλή equal to her father's and in 318 we see this βουλή in action. Here Zeus's mortal child Heracles supplies the βίη while his immortal child Athena supplies the νοῦς.

Nor is the political theme absent from the Keto digression. Hera does not produce hostile sons anymore, but she does rear the Nemean lion to rule (κοιρανέων 331). The Hydra is described as λύγρ' εἰδυῖαν (313) and εἰδυῖαν suggests both Metis (εἰδυῖαν 887) and Prometheus (εἰδώς 559), rivals to Zeus (εἰδώς 545, 550, 561) in knowledge. λύγρα is otherwise confined to the Keto digression (276, 304, 313) and Titanomachy (650, 674). Furthermore, Zeus's thunder and lightning while mentioned are not employed. In fact, these political echoes show how feeble the opposition to Zeus has become. The most Hera can do is cause trouble for Zeus's son by plaguing mankind. The combined force of Typhoeus has now been attenuated into a multitude of lesser monsters. Thus his animal voices have now become embodied: lions are mentioned in only these two sections (321, 323, 327, 833) and the puppies (834, if they are not lion cubs) may look to Cerberus and possibly the bull (832) to Geryon's cattle (and Prometheus' ox).

The Keto digression clearly shows a greater concern for mankind on the part of the gods. With Typhoeus, the incidental result was winds that were disastrous for men. With Heracles mankind is being benefited. The common explanation of his labors, that their goal was to civilize the world for mankind (e.g. Sophocles' *Trachiniae* 1011f, Euripides' *Heracles* 20), may well lie behind Hesiod's presentation. His help is explicit in the case of the Nemean lion, a πῆμ' ἀνθρώποις (329), who ravages the φῦλ' ἀνθρώπων (330). The Lernean hydra "knows grievous things" (313) and this suggests trouble for man, as we know from other sources, for that is the phrase used of Clytaemnestra in the *Odyssey* (11.432).[39] Phix (= Sphinx), too, is an agent of destruction to the Kadmeans (326); the specification of particular men shows not only Hesiod's local bias but also an advance over the generalized reference to mankind found in the Typhoeus episode. Thus in contrast to the incidental destruction from Ty-phoeus' winds (πῆμα μέγα θνητοῖσι 874) we find similar monsters (πῆμ' ἀνθρώποις 329) here defeated because they cause ills for men.

It might be objected that this analysis ignores the role of Beller-ophon and Pegasus, who dispatched one of the monstrous brood, and Perseus, who killed another. Yet Perseus' feat seems to be mentioned only because it produces Chrysaor and Pegasus, and, although Pega-sus is mentioned in two places, this double mention seems to be a structural device for ordering the catalogue.[40] The catalogue's struc-ture also suggests the greater importance of Heracles. It is Heracles who brings to an end each attempt by Keto and Phorcys to produce monsters. They produce Medusa, whose decapitation produces Chry-saor, the father of Geryon, killed along with Orthos and Eurytion by Heracles. Then (295) they produce Echidna, whose children by Ty-phaon—Orthos, Cerberus and finally the Lernean hydra—are all subdued by Heracles. Then they produce the Chimera, whose second child, the Nemean lion, is subdued by Heracles. The chronological difference between the heroes is precise. Pegasus is connected with Medusa's sister not her cousins, and Heracles, great-grandson of Ouranos, appropriately faces the great-grandchildren of Pontos.[41]

Pegasus and Bellerophon are also foils to Heracles. They are both of an earlier generation and they are both heaven-oriented, even if Bellerophon was unsuccessful in his attempt. Heracles' ascent is not mentioned here, although it an important part of the epilogue. Rather we concentrate on Heracles' purely Earth-bound labors, ac-complished without the magical help given Perseus and Bellerophon. Here we have Hera's anger (315), in contrast to its resolution by the marriage of her daughter Hebe to Heracles in the epilogue. Also we should note that the final labors, the ones that suggest Heracles mov-ing beyond the boundaries of mortality are not stated: he is not men-tioned with either the Apples of the Hesperides or Cerberus, labors that go beyond normal geography, the former to the ends of the earth, the latter below it. Thus the Heracles of the Keto catalogue is not the Heracles who gains immortality and life among the gods in the epilogue but a mortal who helps man. While Bellerophon's enemy Chimera is simply described physically, both the Nemean lion and Lernean hydra are elaborated, in terms that suggest Heracles is help-ing mankind. We also find that Heracles is one who works with man;

the same line (317) includes his helper Iolaus and the magnificent epithet emphasizing Heracles' mortality, Ἀμφιτρυωνιάδης.

The close connection between Keto's monstrous brood and Typhoeus suggests the diminution of both the gods' enemies and of Zeus's role in the conflict. Zeus's power is still absolute but he works through agents, his children Athena and Heracles, and the results are much more satisfactory for mankind.

The other narrative digression, the Prometheus episode, marks a mid-point between these two stories in terms of the quality of the contest, the degree of Zeus's involvement and the position of mankind.

### Prometheus

Prometheus, like Typhoeus, is an enemy associated with Hephaestus, here simply by his control of fire.[42] Typhoeus was γυιωθείς (858); now we hear of Ἀμφιγυήεις (i.e., Hephaestus, 571, 579). The παλάμῃσι of Hephaestus were only in a simile in the Typhoeus episode (866) but are now actually employed (580). Once again Hephaestus faces the enemy of Zeus, but here not in a simile but in fact. Hephaestus has developed from a potential enemy of Zeus in the epilogue, to a metaphoric helper in the Typhoeus episode and finally to an actual helper here. Similarly, Gaia before produced the monstrous Typhoeus, enemy of Zeus, whereas now earth (γαίης 571) is that from which monstrous Woman, weapon of Zeus, is produced.

The battle itself involves no force, but is a battle of wits alone, which Zeus wins as decisively as when he fought Typhoeus. Although he at first competes directly (at Mekone), he then simply gives orders to his helpers, Athena and Hephaestus, just as his βίη when used is used indirectly, through the eagle. The Prometheus episode is in fact the culmination of battle by τέχνη.[43] In chronological terms we began with Gaia's τέχνη against Ouranos (160) and then Zeus' versus Kronos (496) and Hera's against Zeus (929).[44] The battle between Prometheus and Zeus is essentially one of τέχνη. The word occurs four times in the episode (540, 547, 555, 560), and the making of the deceptive woman, attractive on the outside but bad within, is precise retribution for Prometheus' crafted offerings, attractively enveloping worthless bones. That Athena and Hephaestus are singled out (in contrast to the story in the *Works and Days*) shows not only Hephaestus' positive role but the resolution of the original antagonism between the two gods (the conflict is all but explicit in 924–929), who are now cooperating. Thus both of them give crowns to the image (576–584).⁴⁵ Hephaestus' crown is particularly interesting because his evil association with a monstrous antagonist such as Typhoeus (recall that he was produced parthenogenically by Hera) is transformed into his making a crown decorated with all the monsters of land and sea (582).⁴⁶ The monsters on the crown are "like living things with voice" (φωνήεσσιν 584) and this recalls Typhoeus, who gave forth all sorts of voices (φωναί 829; the plural is found in only these two places in the poem). Hephaestus' monsters are certainly analogous to the monsters Heracles will have to fight; their use as a decorative element on the first woman suggests their intermediate position between the divine monster Typhoeus and the mortal ones opposing Heracles, just as the first woman is intermediate between the absence of women and the present race of women. All three are called a πῆμα to men: Typhoeus's winds (874), woman (592) and the Nemean lion (329). Significantly, the first two are "great" woes (μέγα πῆμα 874, 592) but the woe has diminished by the time of the Keto digression. Thus the monsters have been reduced to images, conquered by τέχνη, and Zeus's plans are carried out by subordinates, but gods, not men like Heracles. The final step is to have Zeus's divine subordinates give orders to be carried out by men, and this is what we find in the Keto catalogue.

Another indication of the development beyond the Typhoeus episode is that the elements of the Succession Myth while still present are disconnected and trivialized. Here royal honor is not an issue as it was with Kronos (βασιλήιδα τιμήν 462), Metis (βασιλήιδα τιμήν 892) or with Typhoeus, who would have ruled (ἄναξεν 837). Prometheus is called ἄναξ (543) but never βασιλεύς.⁴⁷ The battle is totally mental and concerned not with the division of *timai* among the gods but with the division of an ox between gods and men: ἐκρίνοντο . . . δασσάμενος 535–537 looks to κρίναντο . . . διεδάσσατο 882–885.⁴⁸ There has been concealment (539, 574, 594 cf. 157, 174, 459, 482, 890) and talk (542ff cf. 163ff, 469ff, 890) and grasping out with hands (553 cf. 174, 178, 182, 482, 487, 490), but no one assists the attacker (contrast 168ff, 474ff) and the conflict is not very serious. The concealment in a belly (539, 599, cf. 158, 460, 483, 487, 890, 899) involves only the innards of an ox; the eating is confined to the bees (595) and the eagle (524, eating innards!).⁴⁹

Hesiod seems to have gone out of his way to suppress any indi-

cation of a succession struggle in which Prometheus may originally
have played the important part he is assigned in [Aeschylus'] *Prometheus Bound*. There are several hints of this, the most important being
the odd positioning of the story between the release of the Cyclopes
and that of the Hundred-handers, which are both parts of the Titanomachy. Prometheus is thus placed within the ambit of the Titanomachy,[50] so that the audience might expect to hear of Prometheus
helping Zeus as in the *Prometheus Bound*, but that expectation is dis-
appointed. The prediction of Zeus's dangerous child, Prometheus's
crucial knowledge in the play, is given to Gaia and deferred to the
end of the *Theogony*.

The Prometheus episode is midway between Typhoeus and Keto's brood in terms of mankind as well. Mankind's interests are central
to the story, even if Zeus's side is not yet working for man. Men are
integral to all parts of the story: they are being judged;[51] the fire is
stolen for their benefit as it was withheld to their detriment (564).
The woman is fabricated as an evil for men (570) and she is first
displayed to the assembly of gods and men (586). Yet mankind does
not ultimately benefit, and we do not follow the story of the creation
of the first woman to its conclusion.[52]

So the Prometheus narrative fits well between the Typhoeus and
Keto episodes. The contest for succession is not so clear as in the
Typhoeus episode, nor so totally dissociated from the gods as in the
Keto episode. Zeus's visibility is not so great as in the Typhoeus episode, where he worked directly, forcibly and alone, but not so indirect
as in the Keto episode, where he is not himself present at all but works
through his immortal and mortal children. Finally, mankind is not
the totally incidental victim nor the unambiguous beneficiary of the
action.

Thus the three narrative digressions all fit together in a clear
but complex pattern. The closest to the Titanomachy in terms of
threat from a successor, active participation of Zeus and disregard of
mankind is last in position (Typhoeus) while the farthest removed in
these terms comes earliest in the poem.

As a final check we might consider the chronology of the digressions. We noted earlier that all the digressions seemed to be later than
the Titanomachy; here the question is whether they fit together in
chronology as they do in so many other ways. Indeed they do. The
Typhoeus episode pictures a world without human action, where natural elements like winds are still being created. Tartarus is still a

being, not just a place. In the Prometheus episode, man has been created and is about to be separated from the gods.[53] The catalogue of Keto's brood gives us the present world of a few generations ago.

There are two anomalies but they are only apparent: Typhoeus appears as the mate of one of Keto's children, Echidna (306), even though he was defeated by Zeus in the Typhoeus episode.[54] As we have seen, though, he was relegated to Tartarus, which can be equated with the place under the earth away from gods and men where Echidna's cave is located (301ff) and therefore the mating follows his defeat.[55] Heracles similarly is featured both in the Prometheus episode as killer of the eagle and in the Keto catalogue as killer of several monsters, but since we know Prometheus' punishment lasted for centuries, we can see there is no contradiction.[56] Likewise the apparent contradiction between 526ff where Heracles is said to have freed Prometheus and 616 where Prometheus is said to be bound can be explained by noting that 521–34 is in its content fitted to what precedes since it describes Prometheus's fate in much the way and at about the length as the fates of Menoitios (514–16) and Atlas (517–20).[57] Formal considerations lead to the same conclusion for 521–34 forms its own ring, outside the Prometheus digression, which properly begins at 535:

(b)    Prometheus was bound and his liver eaten, 521–25
(c)    but Heracles stopped this, 526–28
(d)    which was allowed by Zeus to honor Heracles, 529–31
(d)    Zeus honored Heracles, 532
(c)    stopped his anger (χόλος) against Prometheus, 533
(b)    which he had because Prometheus challenged him, 534

(a)    for at Mekone . . . , 535ff
(b)    Prometheus did not avoid Zeus's anger (χόλος) or bonds, 614–16.

Thus the narratives of the *Theogony* are fitted into a complex but elegant structure: the action moves forward in the three succession stories until its programmatic climax in the distribution of *timai* after the Titanomachy. The end point of the program, Zeus's hegemony, is confirmed in the following, non-programmatic description of Zeus's marriages. But at the same time this confirmation contains a new problem, a threat to Zeus's power from a stronger son. It is this threat that is developed in the three non-succession narratives that counter-point the three succession narratives.

There is one final piece to the pattern, one final narrative that has not been discussed and that is the narrative of Hesiod's investiture in the prologue, which shares many of the elements of the non-succession narratives and is the extra-programmatic counterpart to the epilogue of Zeus's marriages.

We noted in chapter 2 how the investiture is marked off from what follows. Critics have argued that this marks a contrast between pastoral setting and poetry as private transaction on the one hand and song with an audience and a public setting on the other.[58] In addition the investiture provides a fitting conclusion to the (reverse) development of digressions in a number of ways. Heracles' benefactions to mankind in the catalogue of Keto's monstrous brood brought us close to the present, but it is only in the investiture, the digression farthest from the epilogue, that we arrive at the narrative present. In the Prometheus digression we heard of mankind in general, in the Keto catalogue of the Kadmeans, but now we hear of one, present-day Kadmean, Hesiod.[59] Secondly, the Muses are clearly subordinates of Zeus, but Zeus is nowhere mentioned in the investiture. The Muses apparently act entirely on their own. But they do not act without mortal assistance, for the poet's assent and activity are required. They gave him the σκῆπτρον and breathed in αὐδὴν θέσπιν but they had to depend on him (i.e., order him) to sing of the gods (33f).[60] Thirdly, the Muses appeared without summons or bribe. Hesiod had not sacrificed to them as one must to Hecate to be rewarded. One might even regard the σκῆπτρον as their bribe to get Hesiod to do something for them.

The final point of development is the most interesting. It involves the succession threat and the perplexing reference to shepherds as "mere bellies."[61] West argues (160) that it is conventional that "the god who appears (or the prophet inspired by him) addresses mankind in strongly derogatory terms." But the parallels he offers, with the exception of Epimenides' adaptation of Hesiod (fr.l), simply show the divinity addressing a foolish mortal. Not only is the provocation in these cases sufficient to explain the rebuke, but none of the examples is an investiture. The one clear parallel for a poet receiving his calling is the story of Archilochus' encounter with the Muses, and here again the Muses react to insult:

When he came to the place which is called Lissides, he thought he saw
women gathered and, thinking they were coming back from the fields
to the city, he approached and mocked them and they received him
with playful laughter.[62]

The possibility remains that the address is best understood in
terms not of conventional action but of the action of the rest of the
poem. Indeed bellies (and wombs) figure prominently in the Kronos
(460,487), Prometheus (539,599) and Metis (890,899) stories and can
be inferred from Gaia's action of placing Kronos λόχῳ (174) to wait
for Ouranos.[63] This might seem fortuitous were there not a surprising number of other elements common to all or most of the (non-
battle) succession narratives. Use of λόγος, persuasive speech, is
found in every case. The Muses shame Hesiod into becoming a poet;
Gaia persuades Kronos to castrate Ouranos; Rhea begs her parents
for help against Kronos; Prometheus tricks Zeus verbally and Zeus
tricks Metis with "wily words" (890). Falseness or trickery is common
to all the stories: the Muses' lies, Kronos' ambush (λόχος) of Ouranos,
the swaddled rock, the deceptive sacrifice of Prometheus, Zeus's tricking of Metis. Something is handed over in all but the swallowing of
Metis: scepter, scythe, rock, dressed-up Woman and fat-wrapped
bones. Hesiod is filled with voice, Kronos is filled first with his children and then with a rock, and the eagle eats the liver (the bees eat
honey). Prophecy figures in the investiture, the overthrow of Kronos
and the birth of Metis. Royal power is clearly the major issue with
Kronos and Zeus and with Zeus and Metis, while Zeus and Prometheus have a royal battle of wits. Hesiod is handed not a ῥάβδος but a
scepter: "the staff carried by kings, priests and prophets" (West 163).
The kingly connection between kings and poets via the Muses is
spelled out later in the prologue. Hesiod's staff also carries prophetic
qualities, as its material (laurel) and its effect (singing what is to be)
show. The emphasis on prophecy at the end of the investiture makes
it plausible that the oak and rock of 35 are Dodona and Delphi.[64] If
so, the rock is not only typologically similar to other rocks in the narratives (the adamantine scythe 162, the swaddled rock 485, the rocks
the Hundred-handers use as weapons (675) but is precisely the rock
that Kronos swallowed, which, when vomited up, was placed in Delphi (500).

The difference between this echo of the succession story and the
echo found in the Prometheus story, is that here the elements fit to-

gether in *no* pattern whatsoever whereas there the pattern was intact even if the elements had been trivialized. The Keto catalogue presents us with echoes that are not completely neutralized as with the investiture story but not so unified as in Prometheus. Walcot (5) has well noted the way the decapitation of Medusa like the castration of Ouranos leads to a new being (Pegasus, Aphrodite), whose name is explained etymologically and who goes to Olympus to join the gods and then has his powers described.[65] One might add that Chrysaor's sword recalls Kronos' scythe; Echidna's cave recalls Kronos' hiding place; and perhaps Geryon's cattle recall Prometheus' divided ox. So we move from trivialization in the Prometheus story, to disjointed but still dangerous elements in the Keto catalogue and finally to the investiture where the elements are both trivialized and arranged in no pattern at all.

A chart of these digressive narratives in order of appearance in the poem will summarize our findings and clarify the basic argument:

| digression | focus on man (decreases) | involvement of Zeus (increases) | succession threat (increases) | chronology (regresses) |
|---|---|---|---|---|
| investiture | Muses give to Hesiod to get him to sing | Muses replace Z; mortals assist | succession story trivialized and broken up | present particular |
| death of Keto's brood | man benefited implicitly | Z's mortal son aided by immortal daughter and man; Pegasus carries Z's lightning | snaky, fiery Typhoeus-like monsters, who rule man | recent past |
| Prometheus | men get meat, fire, women | Z uses only wit, has divine helpers (loses at first!) | succession threat trivialized | separation of gods and men |
| Typhoeus | winds bad for man result | Z fights alone | serious threat to Z's hegemony | post-Titan battle; Tartarus is a person |

A further column could have been added involving death. It is a striking feature of the *Theogony* that the descendants of Phorcys and

Keto are often mortal: their children Medusa and Chimera both die; their grandchildren, the Hydra, the Nemean lion, Orthos and Geryon die. We can see, in fact, that mortality increasingly imbues the digressions the further they are from the epilogue, which offers a distinct contrast: two of Zeus's children by mortal women are immortalized (Heracles, Dionysus). The point is stressed with Semele, ἀϑ-άνατον ϑνητή (942), while Dionysus takes a mortal as wife and she is made immortal by Zeus (949). The section on Zeus' progeny ends with a two-line *gnome* on Heracles' immortality: "happy is he who has done a great deed among the gods and lives (among them) all days ageless and without pain" (954f).[66]

As we move back from the epilogue, mortality intrudes more and more. Typhoeus is crippled, lashed, roasted but apparently not killed but sent to Tartarus (868), where he apparently mates with Echidna (306). Prometheus' punishment gives us a god who is at the same time mortal and immortal—his liver is consumed but regrows daily. Again mankind's mortality is assumed; generation through woman seems to be man's only protection against death.[67] The eagle sent to consume Prometheus' liver is ultimately killed by Heracles—a preparation for his monster-killing role in the Keto digression. The catalogue of Keto's monstrous children is filled with the death of offspring of divine parents (280, 289, 293, 316, 325, 332) and of mortals (326, 330), and mortal Medusa is distinguished from her immortal sisters (277). In the investiture man must worry daily about existence, is a "mere belly" until poetry comes and, as we hear later in the proem, heals the man, "even if he is grieved in heart and has the sorrow of a recent death" (98f).[68]

Thus the investiture gives us the final step in Zeus's absolute control as he works through subordinates against the succession threat and at the same time shows the greatest concern for men, the deepest sense of mortality and the greatest connection of gods and men.[69] We have in the prologue not only the end point in genealogy (Mnemosyne, 54 = 915) but also the end point in Zeus's power and its effect on men. The beginning is also the end, and the movement of the work is toward the Titanomachy in the main narrative and backward away from it to the beginning in the digressions.

Until now it has been useful to describe the movement of program and narrative digressions as a circle in order to keep the differences between the various digressions clear, but we must remember that an audience will comprehend the work from beginning to end and ultimately we need to view the work this way. In linear terms, then, as the main narrative moves chronologically from beginning to middle, the digressions move from end to middle. The result is that the gap decreases steadily between program and digressions until there is almost no difference between the two (Titanomachy, Typhoeus episode). It is probably significant that only here does Hesiod speak of the chronological relationship between two sections.[70] A diagram may make the pattern clearer:

program >
         Ouranos >
                      Kronos >
                                   Titanomachy >
birth of Muses ...............................................epilogue
                         Prometheus >   Typhoeus >
investiture >  Keto's brood >

As the gap is closed, the tension between the three widely separate times of the proem is resolved. Thus, one conclusion of this study can be that the material after 965 does not fit and must have been added later. Presumably someone realizing that the story needed to be brought down to the present but not that the digressions were serving this function just that continued the story beyond its turning point.

As we have seen, the prologue gives us a series of theogonies which ever more closely approximate the basic content of the poem. They are fitted into a hymn to the Muses, the center of which is a narrative of the Muses' birth, while the poem ends with their birth again. The prologue begins, however, with a description of the present activities of the Muses and a narrative of their induction of Hesiod into the role of poet, thereby offering us the chronologically latest point in the poem. Thus we begin with the end point of present celebration and very recent investiture; then we break from that at v.35 to go back to the intermediate past of the birth of the Olympian Muses and their song of Zeus and finally after the hymn to the Muses has been ended we are given the contents of the poem, which represents an expanse of time earlier than the Muses' birth. The bulk of the poem is outlined in the program at the end of the hymn; its epilogue is predicted in the birth narrative in the middle of the hymn; and the end point of its digressions is given in the digressive investiture at the beginning.

# Chapter Five
# SUMMING UP

The first conclusion of this study is that the program outlined at the end of the proem is to be taken seriously. In fact, the primary organizing feature of the poem is the program given in 105–15, which, as we have seen, leads us to expect the genealogies of the children of Ouranos, Night and Pontos, their grandchildren and then how they captured Olympus and distributed their *timai*. The poem follows this format until v.886: after the primordial powers are introduced we hear of the children of Ouranos and Gaia (Titans, Cyclopes, Hundred-handers), ending with the castration of Ouranos that releases the Titans from Gaia's womb; then we have the full list of Night's progeny and their offspring, followed by the children and grandchildren of Pontos, beginning with a long (25 line) catalogue of aquatic divinities whose father is Pontos' eldest child Nereus and ending with the digressive narration of the death of Keto's children. The final portion of the genealogical section, the grandchildren of Ouranos, likewise begins with a long (24 line) catalogue of aquatic divinities, whose father is Ouranos' eldest child Oceanus, and likewise ends with a narrative digression, the Prometheus story. Between the two groups we have the description of Styx's τιμή, the hymn to Hecate and the story of Kronos' defeat. Chiastic structure (children of Ouranos; children and grandchildren of Night; children and grandchildren of Pontos; grandchildren of Ouranos) assures us the genealogical portion of the poem has ended, and then we move to the climactic battle for Olympus. This section too ends with a narrative digression, the Typhoeus episode, after the long description of Tartarus. Thus the program (and the theogonies leading up to it) beside giving us the content of the poem, show that it is divided into two parts, genealogy and politics. Genealogy has given way to politics. Power is no longer to be passed violently from father son but is permanently in the hands of Zeus. Generation is now carefully controlled. The most obvious sign of this is the regular listing of Zeus's progeny at the end of the poem (and the relative absence of other progeny) but an equally impressive demonstration resides in the description of Tartarus, where geography replaces genealogy.

Given the importance of the program, we must wonder why the division of *timai* specified there is not fully narrated. The answer is probably that the usual story of the division between Zeus, Poseidon and Hades is replaced by the much more Zeus-oriented stories of the distribution of *timai* to Styx and Hecate. Zeus uses the promise of *timai* to obtain allies in his upcoming battle against the Titans and he obtains the children of Styx, Victory, Power and Might, who help him both in the Titanomachy proper and in his battle against his father Kronos, which may originally have been part of the same story but was effaced to increase Zeus's glory. We may argue that, since Hecate's honors, too, result from alliance with Zeus, her *timai* involve activities on earth whereas the Titans under whom she first got her honors are relegated to Tartarus. Also, since *timai* generally are described in geographical terms, we may explain the lengthy description of Tartarus as a reflection of Zeus's dispensation: Styx's children aided Zeus and he placed them with him on Olympus; those who fought against Zeus he placed in Tartarus. Thus each of the three non-narrative digressions involves the distribution of *timai* and together they effectively replace the curtailed story of the distribution of *timai* at 885.

Given the program, we must also wonder why the poem continues beyond the distribution of *timai* and conquest of Olympus and why the program does not include certain stories, most notoriously the Typhoeus episode. This question leads us to a second conclusion which is that the three unannounced non-succession stories (the killing of Keto's brood; the tricking of Prometheus; the defeat of Typhoeus), each of which ends a major section of the poem, echo the three succession stories (the castration of Ouranos; the tricking of Kronos; the defeat of the Titans) and furthermore form their own retrograde movement, backward from the narrative present of the proem's investiture through the recent past of Heracles' exploits and the remote past of the separation of men and gods at Mekone to the battle between Zeus and Typhoeus. Thus the odd dismissal of the 'Helikonian' hymn and the second beginning mark two rather distinct chronological points—Hesiod's poetic birth and the birth of Muses (both marked by ποτε)—that are joined only at the end of the poem, in the epilogue, at precisely the point at which the chronological gap between the birth of the Muses and the subject of their song collapses. Such a complex form may seem rather unlikely to us, but only if we judge it by Homeric standards. Pindar, for example, organizes his myths in much the same way, giving us either the end point or the mid point at the beginning of the myth and then working forward toward it.[1] Hesiod has simply done this twice: the Olympian Muses singing to Zeus represents the chronological midpoint, which is reached at the poem's end; Hesiod's investiture represents the chronological end point, which comes at the poem's beginning. The reason is obvious: it is at the midpoint that Zeus's glory is greatest.

A final confirmation of the validity of such a structure is that it is very much like what we find in Hesiod's other great poem, *The Works and Days*—composition by juxtaposed blocks.

# Part II

# The *Works and Days*

## Chapter Six
## INTRODUCTION TO PART II

While there seems to be endless critical fascination with the myths in the first part of the *Works and Days*, the second half, the almanac-like set of injunctions about farming and sailing, has been overlooked, partially because it gives the impression of being 'just facts' but more significantly because it appears to be a mostly incoherent jumble of maxims with only the most superficial formal order.[1] The poem begins with a hymn and invocation (1–10) followed by a description of the two Erides (11–26)[2] and Hesiod's dispute with his brother Perses (27–41). We then have two myths, Prometheus/Pandora (42–105) and the Ages of Man (106–201), followed by a fable (202–12). After a long section of moral injunctions (213–382), the description of the farmer's activities, which I shall call the "Almanac," begins and at its end, we hear about sailing (618–94, the "Nautilia"). Another set of prescriptions (695–764) leads to the final section, a list of lucky and unlucky days (765–828). The most recent commentator, M.L. West, speaks for many when he concludes (44) that there is little pattern to the poem:

> Did he envisage at the outset a poem which should begin with a series of stories and homilies to Perses and the kings, pass on to instruction on husbandry, then deal with sailing, then dissolve into a jumble of assorted advice, and lastly treat of the days of the month? The answer is surely no. Such a plan has little logic and less beauty.

Roughly speaking, criticism of the form of the *Works and Days* has gone through three stages.[3] During the nineteenth century, the tendency was to extract from the poem a purer, more unified core and to treat everything else as either an interpolation or an addition.[4] Early in the twentieth century, a reaction set in to this patently subjective procedure, and critics began arguing either that the poem could be explained by appeal to a particular genre (the wisdom poetry of Theognis and Solomon; more recently, the paraenetic tradition seen in Nestor's speeches in the *Iliad*) or that the whole was bound together by one or two major themes such as justice and work, to which every element could be subordinated.[5] In the last few decades, critics have become increasingly uncomfortable with such reductionistic solutions to the problem of order:

Wollte man . . . schliessen, dass die Erkenntnis der Einheit dieses Ged-
ichtes sich nun endgültig Bahn gebrochen hat, so würde man sich
gründlich irren. Zwar findet die analytische Liedertheorie keine An-
hänger mehr, aber ernste Versuche, den Zusammenhang des Ganzen
gründlich und im einzelnen zu erklaren, sind noch kaum unternom-
men worden. (Verdenius 111)

Recent critics have arranged the poem into patterns of repeated
themes (Blusch), phrases (Walcot) or rhetorical modes (Nicolai,
Schmidt), but these are usually too abstract and subjective to be persuasive.[6] Some appeal to a (usually Homeric) paradigm lying behind
the poem, such as the argument between Achilles and Agamemnon
(Munding), the "Paris Song" said to be embedded in the *Iliad* (Peabody) or the beggars' quarrel in *Odyssey* 18 (Nagy).[7] More commonly
scholars speak of the "stream" of Hesiod's thought, which flows along
a path of associations,[8] but the problem with the associative view is
that one need presume only one link to connect anything with anything else and so such a method is even less useful in explaining the
details of the poem than the reductive unity of the earlier generation
of scholars.[9] The peculiar state of literary study of the poem is
marked by the fact that West in his recent edition combines, to reviewers' approbation, all three stages, recognizing both that "mental
association is an important factor" and that the poem minus the two
myths, Almanac and Nautilia, "reduces itself almost entirely to an
alternation between 'Dike prospers' and 'Hybris is punished', or between the advantages of work and the disadvantages of idleness" (47).
At the same time he returns us to the nineteenth century view except
that he allows Hesiod himself to have made the interpolations and
additions:

> It is a poem which grew in scope as Hesiod composed it. . . . If the
> poem had ended at 264 or 316 or 380 or 617 or 688 or 764 . . . we
> should have been just as satisfied that it was complete as we are now. [10]

It is important to realize how this differs from his earlier criticism,
that the whole "has little logic and less beauty." Now we are considering the audience's perception of the poem as it proceeds. A logic and
beauty derived from concerted, repeated study of a poem is quite
different from the path of an audience's expectations. We will want to
address both criticisms.

There is reason to think that critics have been overly pessimistic
in their evaluation of the poem's form. First, paradoxical though it

may seem, the parts are *too* 'disorderly.' Patterns are established only to be destroyed, and our expectations are repeatedly frustrated. Since the Prometheus/Pandora story follows its model in the *Theogony*, we expect Zeus's threat of an evil gift to end with the acceptance of Pandora into Prometheus' house, and this is surely the implication of Prometheus' warning to refuse Zeus's gift. After all, Pandora is the one from whom, the *Theogony* tells us, the evil race of women came. However, it is only when she opens a mysterious pithos which has suddenly entered the story that she causes any trouble, and she seems to do this of her own volition (95), not because of Zeus's plan.[11] The story was supposed to show the gods hiding βίος (42) but instead Zeus hides fire (50) and Pandora scatters grievous cares (95); that is, she reveals evil instead of hiding good.[12] The Ages Myth offers an egregious structural problem when its list of metallic ages is interrupted by an age of heroes (156–73), which many critics say is inserted simply to square with Homer.[13] The fable surprises us by being addressed to the kings rather than Perses despite Hesiod's programmatic statement in v.10 that Perses will be his addressee, itself already compromised by the generalized νήπιοι introducing the Prometheus myth (40). Also the fable leaves us confused since it has no moral, other than the implicit one that might makes right, just the reverse of what Hesiod wishes to tell the kings, and, as a final dissonance, what follows is addressed to Perses not the kings.[14]

If we turn to the Almanac and Nautilia, the so-called "Calendar," we find ourselves similarly confused. I do not refer to the massive chaos of the gnomic material, for which scholarship does not yet have adequate analytical equipment, but cases where simple patterns have been disrupted. The Almanac begins with the date for plowing. Then Hesiod harangues Perses about begging (394ff), though before he was not a beggar but a litigant, an apparent inconsistency which has provided the cornerstone of many arguments against the poem's unity.[15] After some further injunctions to the farmer, Hesiod gives us a quite different date and a long description of wood-cutting for wagon and plow (414–36). Only then do we return, with yet another date, to the time for plowing (448) and then jump ahead in the calendar to discuss spring plowing (462).[16] The chronology so far has been merely confused, but it is actually overturned when at the end of the Almanac Hesiod interrupts his description of harvesting the grain and vintage (564ff) with a chronologically anomalous description of summer relaxation (582–96).[17] In a similar fashion Hesiod interrupts his advice about sailing (618ff) with a long "superimposed layer" (West 55) of digression about his travel to the funeral games of Amphidamas in Chalcis (646–62). A "free-wheeling" (West 45) set of maxims follows, which appears to have been arbitrarily separated from the equally random set before the Almanac discussing many of the same subjects. As Nicolai (163) notes, this is not the only place where "zusammenhörige Blocke" are "absichtlich getrennt." The "Days" section, which ends the poem, has three different time schemes and no obvious order, despite the availability of a simple chronological frame. It almost seems as if the poet took perverse pleasure in confusing his audience.

Critics have studied the problems of the first part, especially the myths, with considerable intensity and have often found meaning behind the apparent chaos. For example the Heroic Age by disrupting the pattern of metallic Ages at the same time shows that the downward trend of the Ages is not absolute but dependent on the group's actions: the Heroic Age is "juster and better" (158) and therefore has a better end.[18] This is presumably a message to the present Iron Age that life *can* be better if people are just. Likewise, although the fable has no immediate moral, one is presented sixty lines later (276ff), and critics have seen that the delay gives additional force to the intervening exhortations to justice.[19] One can deduce important critical principles from these examples: in the Ages myth egregious disorder masks larger order; in the fable the audience's expectation is kept unfulfilled for over sixty lines. It will be our task to apply these principles to the neglected second part of the poem.

A second reason to be encouraged is that there are occasional hints of a grand design. Hesiod ends the description of the two Erides with the statement that good Eris leads potters and carpenters to fight and, in a odd collocation, leads "beggar to envy beggar, singer to envy singer" (πτωχὸς πτωχῷ φθονέει καὶ ἀοιδὸς ἀοιδῷ 26).[20] Hesiod then advises Perses to give up his lawsuit, resist bad Eris and turn to good Eris and work. The Almanac begins, as we have noted, with the picture of Perses as a beggar (πτώσσῃς 395), quite to the consternation of the critics, and the digression of the Nautilia pictures Hesiod as a poet (cf ἀοιδῆς 659), striving with poets. So the model given in v.26 is first disturbed by having beggar (Perses) fight with poet (Hesiod) but ultimately resolved in the picture of poet (Hesiod) competing with other poets. Also, the first myth is introduced by the statement that if things were different man could hang his rudder over the fire-

place quickly (πηδάλιον . . . ὑπὲρ καπνοῦ 45) while the Nautilia begins with the injunction to hang the rudder over the fireplace (πηδάλιον . . . ὑπὲρ καπνοῦ 629).[21] In at least two cases, then, distinctive
echoes—these are the only references to poets, beggars and rudders—lead us forward in the poem until the Nautilia.[22] A further
distinctive correspondence is that the Almanac begins with instruc-
tions to cut wood for a wagon and to avoid breaking one's plow (423–
36) while the Nautilia ends with a warning about the danger of breaking one's wagon by overloading it (693f), even though this has nothing to do with sailing.[23] The word for axle (ἀξόνη) occurs in only these
two places in the poem (424, 693) while verbs meaning "break" occur
only in this environment (434, 440, 666, 693, this last being perhaps
a triple pun: ἄμαξαν . . . ἀξόνα καυάξαις). These three examples of
distinctive repetition share the further feature of occurring at what
seem to be crucial structural points—end of proem, beginning of first
myth, beginning of Almanac, beginning and end of Nautilia—and
we should feel encouraged to look for further structurally significant
echoes to reinforce them.

At the same time, we must recognize that these correspon-
dences, while suggesting a level of control not ordinarily credited to
the poet, do not answer West's objection that the poem could stop
anywhere, unless we wish to argue that the description of the wagon
(423–26) since it precedes the description of the plow (427–36), creates a dissonance (one plows before one harvests with a wagon) that
is resolved only when the activities of plowing and harvesting are
given in the correct order, in the Almanac.[24] Nor are the correspon-
dences rhetorically significant; excepting perhaps the case of poet
and beggar, the audience has not been waiting for any expectation to
be fulfilled.[25] Finally, they are isolated and, unless they can be supported by a number of cogent additional echoes, there is the danger
that the echoes are random.[26]

Still we may feel encouraged by these findings to approach the
poem in greater detail and hope to challenge West's judgments and
Edwards' conclusion (192) that the structure is "loosely-knit and un-
systematic" and that there is "exceedingly little in the way of internal
cross-references."[27] We will want to look for thwarted expectation,
correspondence over distance, and structural articulation. Also, unlike most previous studies, we will be looking for repetitions of things
(e.g. rudders) more than ideas (e.g. justice), images more than concepts, nouns more than verbs and, to avoid the everpresent danger

of subjectivity, we will try to insist that the repetitions be distinctive, so that we do not falsely emphasize a few convenient occurrences while ignoring the rest.

Since the *Works and Days* explicitly alludes to the *Theogony* in its reference to the (incorrect) doctrine that there is only one Eris (11) and since it is probably his recitation of the *Theogony* at the games of Amphidamas that Hesiod describes in WD 655–59, it is not surprising that the *Works and Days* follows the form of the *Theogony*, with its invocation and program. The invocation and hymn of *Theogony* 1–103, involving praise of the Muses, culminates in a clear statement of the relationship between god and poet (δότε δ' ἱμερόεσσαν ἀοιδήν 104), which leads to the program that the Muses are to sing (κλείετε . . . γένος . . . οἳ . . . εἴπατε δ' ὡς . . . εἴπαθ' ὅτι). Likewise the invocation and hymn of the *Works and Days*, involving praise of Zeus, culminates in a clear statement of the relationship between god and poet (ἴθυνε θέμιστας / τύνη· ἐγὼ δέ κε Πέρσῃ ἐτήτυμα μυθησαίμην 9f).[28] What follows is the core of what Hesiod has to tell his brother, marked as such at both beginning (Πέρσῃ ἐτήτυμα μυθησαίμην 10) and end (ὦ Πέρσῃ, σὺ δὲ ταῦτα τεῷ ἐνικάτθεο θυμῷ 27).[29] The description of the two Erides, then, is our program and our first task will be to see what it teaches us about the structure of the poem.[30] Judging from the *Theogony*, digressions will be important and Hesiod will not simply follow the program but ring variations contrapuntally on it.

## Chapter Seven

# THE PROGRAM

Although the importance of the description of the two Erides has rarely been doubted, scholars have generally assumed that they are to be equated with justice/injustice and work/idleness and that these two themes alternate throughout the poem, though justice dominates the first part and work the second.[1] Thus they say that while the myth of Prometheus and Pandora begins with the loss of *bios* and the consequent need for work (i.e., good Eris), it ends with the beginning of death and disease for man and the conclusion that one cannot fool Zeus, and so the bad Eris represented by Prometheus' struggle against Zeus led to destruction.[2] Similarly the Ages myth describes a degeneration of the social and moral fabric in terms of injustice (bad Eris), but the rewards of the Golden and Heroic Ages are spoken of in terms of a paradise with abundant *bios* (good Eris). The fable of the hawk and nightingale may have nothing to do with livelihood and work, but it is followed by a description of the just city reminiscent of the paradise enjoyed by the Golden and Heroic Ages (καρπὸν δὲ φέρει ζείδωρος ἄρουρα 237 = καρπὸν . . . φέρει ζείδωρος ἄρουρα 172–73 = καρπὸν δ' ἔφερε ξείδωρος ἄρουρα 117), and then a series of injunctions for justice (248–92) and for work (298–316). Although such an analysis probably has some validity, one must concur with Verdenius (112) that it tells us little about the details of the poem: "verdecken sie die tatsächliche Buntheit des Inhalts."

What scholars have not noted is that the first part of the poem (until v.286) describes war and strife while its few descriptions of livelihood and work are all cast in ambiguous terms, limited to describing the way things used to be or ideally might be.[3] Now the half is better than the whole (40); *bios* has been lost because of Prometheus (47f); earth produced grain automatically only after death and only in the Golden Age (117f) and still produces it only for some of the heroes after their deaths (172f);[4] the rewards of the just city are predominantly non-agricultural: half a line is devoted to earth's produce, which seems to be produced without work while two and a half to the oak and sheep (232–34).[5] That is, to the degree that livelihood is discussed at all in the first part, it is the ideal *bios* provided by the *gods* in the *past* and not what *man* can obtain for himself in the *present*.[6]

Similarly the word "work" (ἔργον) which is emphasized in the description of good Eris (20, 21) and then said to be what bad Eris keeps Perses from (28) is not found in the singular again in the first part although it occurs with great frequency in the second (311, 316, 382, 409, 412, 422, 440, 443, 444, 554, 578, 579, 779). The verb "work" is never used in the first half except for the hypothetical condition if the gods had not hidden *bios* (43) and to refer to the Bronze Age killers who "worked in bronze" (151).[7] In the second part, the verb is used repeatedly, usually of farm work (299, 309, 312, 314, 382, 397, 438, 623, 827). The noun form does occur in the plural in the first part but never in the sense of a farmer's work except for another hypothetical condition: if the gods had not hidden *bios*, the work (ἔργα) of the oxen and mules would have been destroyed (46). Otherwise we hear primarily of σχέτλια ἔργα (124, 238, 254), an adjective particularly associated with bad Eris (15, cf. 187, accounting for all its uses in the poem) or the works of war (146), of Athena (64) and twice the plural is used of the food eaten at a feast (119, 231). This is in sharp opposition to the second half of the poem, which hardly mentions war or strife at all and deals with precisely what ἔργα man can do and what he can obtain for himself in the present (306, 308, 334, 393, 398, 454, 494, 641, 767, 773).

So, rather than alternating throughout the poem, the themes of the two Erides seem to define the two major parts of the poem.[8] If this can be substantiated in detail, we will be able to answer the complaint of West and others that the poem could stop anywhere, for the audience will expect to hear about good Eris as well as bad.

Our first task, then, is to see how well the description of bad Eris matches the first part of the poem and good Eris the second. Embedded in this procedure is the assumption that the poem divides into two parts, with the new introduction beginning at v.286 and the Calendar proper (i.e., Almanac plus Nautilia) at v.383, but since this is generally accepted, even by critics who divide the poem into many more parts, we should not be unduly concerned, and, as we will see, there are ample formal grounds for the separation.[9]

### A. Bad Eris

Hesiod begins his program by saying "there was not, after all (ἄρα), one kind of Eris" (11). It is commonly recognized that he is referring to and correcting *Theogony* 225ff, where only one kind of

Eris, Ἔρις στυγερή, was mentioned.[10] If we are right in saying that the poem moves from bad Eris to good Eris, we might expect to find the first part of the poem reproducing the environment of the *Theogony*. This expectation is almost immediately fulfilled by the Prometheus/Pandora myth, which closely echoes the Prometheus myth in the *Theogony*. Critics sometimes attribute this echo to Hesiod's barren mythic imagination but it has the positive function of reaffirming, for those who know the *Theogony*, the equation bad Eris = world of *The theogony*.[11] We have the same dialogue between Zeus and Prometheus in both myths, the same creation of woman and similar results for men.[12] The two obvious changes are the introduction of the foolish brother, Epimetheus, and the story of the pithos, which replaces the generation of women as the cause of man's troubles.[13] The first change clearly reflects Hesiod's dispute with his brother[14] while the second introduces a paradigm that re-echoes throughout the poem, as we will see. A third change is the absence of any mention of the dispute at Mekone, which started the rivalry between Zeus and Prometheus. Vernant cunningly argues that it has been replaced by the dispute between Hesiod and Perses.[15]

The Ages myth also recalls the world of the *Theogony* while offering a polar opposition to its partner, the Prometheus myth. It is introduced as "another story," with presumably the same moral and the same rhetorical force as the Prometheus myth. Its content is in a general way the same also for "how gods and men are born from the same source (ὁμόθεν 108)," supposes the same initial unity of gods and men as the Prometheus story with its derivation of the first woman from Pandora and also its definition of Mekone as the time "when the gods and men were being separated (ἐκρίνοντο Th.535)."[16] Despite these similiarities the two myths are opposed in several ways. The Prometheus/Pandora myth dealt with individuals and concentrated on the dealings between gods; the change for man was sudden and went from a life of ease to hardship and death. The Ages myth shows groups of men, interacting among themselves; the change is gradual and in one case, the Heroic Age, leads from war and death to eternal bliss. At the same time the Ages myth is clearly meant to carry the story of man on down to the present. As we moved in the *Theogony* from the aboriginal powers and their offspring such as Night and Eris to the Titans and finally to the Olympians, so here we move from Eris the daughter of Night to the Titan Prometheus and then to the Ages, where Zeus takes over from Kronos (138 vs. 111).[17]

The ¨st part of the *Works and Days*, then, presents a history of man that parallels the *Theogony*'s history of the gods.[18]

Thus the two main λόγοι in their own ways both recall the *Theogony* and this suggests that bad Eris is like the world of the *Theogony*, a suggestion confirmed by the description of bad Eris, where the emphasis is on war, the gods and honor. Taking the description as programmatic, we are led to expect three themes in the first part of the poem: (a) war and strife (ἡ μὲν γὰρ πόλεμόν τε κακὸν καὶ δῆριν ὀφέλλει 14); (b) plans of the gods (ἀθανάτων βουλῇσιν 16; βουλή is a key phrase in the *Theogony* as we have seen); (c) honor but not friendship (οὔ τις τήν γε φιλεῖ βροτός, ἀλλ' . . . τιμῶσι 15f).[19]

War and strife dominate the two myths and the fable: we move from strife between gods (Zeus and Prometheus) to strife between men (Bronze, Heroic, Iron Ages) to strife between animals (in the fable).[20] Conversely, we hear nothing of war or strife in the second half, except for a brief allusion to the Trojan War in the Nautilia, which is explicitly contrasted with the present, peaceful, nearby contest of Hesiod.[21] The Calendar gives us a complex and harmonious, albeit limited, social interaction between men: Perses is now a beggar (396) and not engaged in a legal dispute; oxen are not to fight (439); men are to pay attention to their jobs (410, 444f, 448, 458f, 502); cooperation is encouraged (295, 345, 469–71, 708, 712). The words for violence and justice, ὕβρις and δίκη, are confined to the first part.[22]

As for the plans of the gods, although the gods appear in both parts of the poem, in the first part they have a purpose and will and it is from their vantage point that we often look, as in the *Theogony*, whereas in the Almanac and Nautilia the gods, when present at all— and that is not very often—are simply the random factor in the worker's routine. They are not the focus of attention.[23] In the first part, even outside the myths which they dominate, they are often the subject, acting upon man (Zeus 5–9, 18, 229, 239, 242, 247, 267, 273, 276, 281; Oath 219, Justice 260). The term βουλή is confined to the first part (16, 79, 99, 122, cf. 245) and refers only to Zeus, with one exception, 266, where Zeus is mentioned in the next line. In the Calendar, however, the gods are usually meteorological (383, 416, 417, 488, 506, 518, 547, 553, 566, 572, 587, 594, 598, 609f, 615, 619) or manifested in natural objects like "grain of Demeter" or "gift of Dionysus" (393, 430, 464, 466, 521, 597, 614). We find them as subject only five times: "works, which the gods marked out for man" (398, referring back to the Prometheus myth); "if the Olympian one should give good" (474); "poverty which Zeus gives men" (638); "the Muses taught me" (662); "if Poseidon is not friendly or if Zeus wishes to destroy" (667f). The Days belong to Zeus (765, 769), but aside from two references to the past (birth of Apollo 771, of Horkos 804) the gods do not appear.[24] In the Calendar (minus the Days) man's relationship to the gods is confined to an isolated reference to prayer (465) and Hesiod's dedication to the Muses (658) whereas in the first part it was assumed as the norm—the Silver Age neglect of the gods caused their demise (135f) and the same cause will destroy the Iron Age (187) while the vengeful gods stand behind all the injunctions to justice.

The first part of the poem is also distinguished from the second part by the presence of honor, which implies hierarchy, and the absence of friendship, which implies equality. τιμή occurs only in 16, 138, 142, 173c, always of the relationship between gods and men. As for τιμή among men, the natural recipients would be the kings. In the *Theogony* kings are the representatives of Zeus (honored by the Muses! 81), but in the *Works and Days* that relationship has been disturbed and they no longer, like Zeus, care for straight justice and their honor now is described as "gift-eating."[25] The kings disappear after the first part and giving takes on a different coloration: no longer is it a "bribe" one gives to a superior but an offering or present one gives to a neighbor.[26] One honors a superior while one is friend to an equal, and not surprisingly φιλία does not occur with τιμή: we honor but do not love bad Eris (15f) and the only times φιλία occurs in the first part describe the close relationship between the Golden Age and the gods (120, bracketed by West) or the impending lack of φιλία among brothers that will mark the end of the present generation (184). Conversely, friendship is frequently mentioned in the second part, especially in the injunctions surrounding the Calendar: 300, 306, 309, 342, 353, 360, 370, 608, 712, 713, 788.

## B. Good Eris

Turning to the program outlined in the description of good Eris (20–26), we find (1) an emphasis on making even the feckless (ἀπάλαμον) man work, (2) a description of the wealthy man who hastens to plow and grow (i.e., farm both seed and plant crops),[27] organizes his house and amasses wealth, causing envy in his neighbor[28] and finally (3) competition between potters, carpenters, beggars and singers. Thus work replaces war, competition of equals replaces hierarchical honor and envy replaces the plans of the gods.[29] Most important, the individual is now acting on himself rather than others. This program is realized in the second part.

It can hardly be doubted that the whole impetus of the Calendar is to urge diligence and forethought so as not to be ἀπάλαμον. Critics have even made this theme the dominant one of the whole poem, but the importance of the other elements of the program needs to be recognized.[30] For example, the specification of plant crops as well as seed crops (ἀρώμεναι ἠδὲ φυτεύειν 22) is fully borne out in the Almanac where we hear at first only of grain ( = seed) but ultimately of viticulture ( = plant) as well. Critics as early as Steitz (27) noted that this is meant to represent "das Ganz des Landbaues" and that it looks to "der Inhalt des grosseren Theiles des Gedichts, von 286 an." We may suspect that polarity is again at work, as we saw with the two myths and will see again with the Almanac ( = farmer) and Nautilia ( = sailor): grain and grape, bread and wine, Demeter and Dionysus are, at least by the time of Euripides (*Bacchae* 274ff), recognized as a natural as well as supernatural pair and it is probably no accident that these two gods are mentioned at the end of the Almanac, both in terms of their products (597, 614).[31]

Further there are several related themes from the programmatic description of good Eris which appear only in the second part of the poem: house, need, wealth, beggars and singers.

Whereas city (πόλις) is mentioned almost exclusively in the first part (222, 227, 240, 269, 527), house (οἶκος) is mentioned repeatedly in the Almanac (395, 405, 407, 428, 432, 495, 523, 525, 601) and Nautilia (627, 673) and in the injunctions surrounding them (325, 364f, 376, 695, 733, 800) but rarely in the first part. The occurrences in the first part are all negative: in the unjust city the houses are reduced (244); the Silver Age stays at home in its long infancy (131) and the Bronze Age has bronze houses (150). The verb χατίζω ("need") is found only twice in the poem: in the program (21) and at the beginning of the Almanac (394) in the same position in the line; the verb χρηΐζω ("need") occurs only in the second part of the poem (317, 351, 367, 500, 634, cf 404); and λιμός ("hunger") is found only there (299, 302, 363, 404, 647) and in the description of the just and unjust cities (230, 243). The evils sustained after Zeus hid *bios* and in the various Ages do not involve need.

One might equate the wealthy man described in the program with the Hesiod of the first part, whose property is being sought by his brother, but, since Perses has more than his share, this is unlikely. It is more likely that this description looks forward to the second part and the position of plenty the farmer is expected to have: he has the means to get oxen and hired help (405f); someone else will come to ask *him* for wagon and oxen (453f). He is in the position to measure generously for his neighbor (349) and even give gifts (354ff). He is not so driven by poverty that he has to resort to sailing.

The group of competitors referred to in 25f is at first glance perplexing, but we ultimately find in the second part that the beggar is Perses and the poet is Hesiod. The first two competitors, potter and carpenter, are closely allied: both work with their hands on material and produce artifacts, artifacts which are prominent in the second half of the poem: pithos, plow, wagon, house. The addition of singer suggests that the group should be defined as itinerant professionals,[32] though it seems unlikely that a potter would move far from his kiln. The addition of the beggar at first glance renders all attempts at order hopeless, but when we come to the only other mention of beggars, at the beginning of the Almanac, we find that the beggar's useless νομός of words (403) is opposed to the farmer's νόμος of the fields (388) [33] and that the beggar is said to speak many vain things (402).

The beggar, then, is a man of words, not deeds like the potter and carpenter, and so is fittingly joined with the singer. Peabody even goes so far as to interpret the *Works and Days* as a "Competition Song" sung by Hesiod against Perses, using as his basis the quarrel between Odysseus and the beggar Iros in *Odyssey* 18, while Svenbro has developed the intriguing thesis of "belly poets" who must sing for their meals (cf. *Theogony* 26) as opposed to the later, more independent professionals.[34] This is rather speculative but it is surely significant that the only beggar mentioned in the *Works and Days* is Perses and that he is mentioned at the beginning of the Almanac, for the only (human) singer is Hesiod himself, and he is described in competition with other singers at the funeral games of Amphidamas, in the middle of the Nautilia. The contrast between beggar and singer given as the last item of the program takes us from the beginning of the Almanac almost to the end of the Nautilia, even though there has been no talk of sailing in the program. The court case between Hesiod and Perses (bad Eris) before the crooked kings has been replaced by the contest between Hesiod and other poets (good Eris) before the (kingly?) sons of Amphidamas. Contest replaces war in both program and poem.[35] Hesiod's dedication of his victory tripod is the most strik-ing sign of honor to the gods in either part. Hesiod is even said to speak the mind of Zeus (661), which is obscure to other mortals (483f).

Given this contrast between Perses the beggar and Hesiod the poet, we may now be in a position to address a problem that has per-plexed critics: the reference to Perses as δῖον γένος (299). The phrase δῖον γένος should mean that Perses is descended from Zeus,[36] but critics have been unable to make sense of that. West (232) adopts Wi-lamowitz's suggestion that "their immigrant father had represented himself to the Boeotians as a descendant of the nobles who had gone out to found the Aeolian colonies generations before." He notes that kings were said to come from Zeus "but Perses' social status is low (214)." There is, however, another group said to if not be descended from at least come from Zeus (πρὸς Διός),[37] beggars (Od.14.58), and Perses is definitely a beggar.[37] This address comes at the beginning of the second part of the poem and one may even wonder whether He-siod is replacing the hierarchically defined kings, descended from Zeus (cf. Th.96) with the need-defined beggar Perses.

Equally as important as the particular references for beggars and singers is the general sense of the whole list. Critics have been understandably disturbed that we hear of envy and anger with good Eris since these seem to be qualities more appropriate to bad Eris.[38] But if we compare these to the war and strife of bad Eris we may see the essential difference: with bad Eris the effects of pitting man against man are external while the effect of the competition described for good Eris has only internal effect: potters do not rob each other's pithoi; carpenters do not destroy each other's houses. Thus, for ex-ample, gifts in the first part are viewed externally (to be "eaten") while in the second part we hear of their psychological effect on the recipi-ent (360). Also war and strife necessitate constant interaction with others (friends and enemies); competition produces only casual and occasional contact and, at least for the potter and carpenter, the in-dividual is involved with an object. Sufficient livelihood offers the pos-sibility of court cases in the first part (33), the possibility of trading overseas in the second part.

Thus the two Erides by their polarities define in many ways the content of the two major parts of the poem, separated at v.286. This point of division is not arbitrary. In the first place the address to Perses in 286 differs from the others in several ways. Perses is called a μέλα νήπιε only in 286 and 633,[39] and only in 286 and 397 does Hesiod set himself in relation to Perses by name. In 286 alone we have the poet describing the content of his exhortation as he did at the very beginning of the poem.[40] In terms of content, Heath (250) has well noted that in 289f we have "the most emphatic statement yet of the necessity of work" for "κακότης and ἀρετή are not 'vice' and 'virtue' but inferior and superior standing in society, determined principally by wealth." This is a radical revision of the terminology of the first part of the poem, with its focus on justice; for instance, in 193 ἀρείονα means "stronger" not "socially more prominent" and in 240 the κακός is "evil" not "socially inferior."

The division at 286 is formally articulated as well, most obviously by the echoes of the beginning of the first part which can be found in 286–326. Demeter is mentioned in both (300,32); ὡραίου βιότου 307 recalls βίος ὡραῖος 31f; ἁρπακτά 320 recalls ἁρπάζων 38; the envy of wealth in 312 recalls 22f as ἀλλοτρίων κτεάνων 315 echoes κτήμασ' ἐπ' ἀλλοτρίοις 34; the two roads (288f) and the double αἰδώς (316–19) recall the two Erides. The statement that the gods easily dim the shameless (325f) recalls the invocation of Zeus (especially ῥεῖα . . . μινύθουσι δὲ οἶκον 325 and ῥεῖα δ' ἀρίζηλον μινύθει 6).[41] The terms are the same but the view is now from a different direction: earlier Perses was not allowed to listen in court because he lacked *bios*; now he is told to work so that Demeter may fill his basket with βίοτος; before he was allied with the gift-eating kings; now he is compared to the drones who eat the bees' labor without work (304–6). Perses as litigant tried to steal *bios* from Hesiod; Perses as beggar tries to get it from him by begging. The basic situation in both cases is the same: Perses does not have *bios*; all that has changed is the means he will use. The contrast in Perses' role is a token of the difference in the two sections: "Hesiod stations [Perses] in his poem as he chooses."[42]

The sense of a new beginning at v.286 comes not only from the echoes of the beginning of the first part and from Perses' new role as beggar but also from the strong formal closure that marks off the first part. The first part is articulated by its stories and the moral imperatives which follow: there are three stories (two myths and a fable) and three sets of imperatives involving δίκη: ἄκουε Δίκης (213, addressed to Perses); καταφράζεσθε . . . δίκην (248f, to the kings) and Δίκης ἐπάκουε (275 to Perses again).[43] Each set of imperatives matches one of the stories in such a way that the first set recalls to a degree the Prometheus story, the second clearly echoes the Ages myth and the third set gives the answer to the perplexing fable and therefore marks the end of the whole section.[44]

The relationship between story and imperatives is clearest with the fable, which lacks the needed moral (that might does *not* make right) and so creates in the audience an unfulfilled expectation until, sixty lines later, Hesiod tells Perses (not the kings!) that Zeus has established the *nomos* for fish, beasts and birds that they eat each other but for man he has given justice instead (276–80). As we have seen, the connection between Zeus's *nomos* and the fable has often been remarked; what has not been noticed is that the intervening two sets of imperatives, first to Perses about hybris and the just and unjust cities (213–47) and then to the kings about the guarantors of justice (248–73), answer the myths preceding the fable. This is more obvious with the message to the kings since the 30,000 watchers are clearly the members of the Golden Age who became earthly *daimones*, mortal guardians (φύλακες θνητῶν ἀνθρώπων 123 = 253). If 124f are not interpolated from 254f, as West and Solmsen think, then the equation is even stronger for the two lines will be the fullest repetition within the poem.[45] The watchers guard against those who do not revere the gods (θεῶν ὄπιν οὐκ ἀλέγοντες 251) and this phrase recalls those of the Silver and Iron Ages (οὐδὲ θεῶν ὄπιν εἰδότες 187; cf. οὐδ' ἀθανάτους θεραπεύειν 135).[46] Hesiod then speaks of the maiden Justice going to Zeus (256) and we recall the threat of the virginal Aidos and Nemesis leaving earth (200).[47] Hesiod ends the section praying not to be just if injustice is rewarded, and this recalls his (unrealized) wish not to be a member of the Iron Age (νῦν δὴ ἐγὼ μήτ' 270 = μηκέτ' . . . ἐγὼ . . . νῦν γὰρ δή 174–6).

Since the third set of imperatives answers the fable and the second recalls the Ages myth, we should not be surprised that the first recalls the Prometheus myth. The fool who recognized evil too late (218) is clearly Epimetheus, whose name means just that, while the picture of justice crying through the city bringing evil to men (κακὸν ἀνθρώποισι φέρουσα 223) recalls the sicknesses let out of the pithos, bringing evil to men (κακὰ θνητοῖσι φέρουσαι 103), and the woe Zeus brings (πῆμα 242) recalls the woe he brought to Prometheus (πῆμα 82) as opposed to the *bios* he hid and which the just city has (232 = 42).

The relationship between the three stories and the three sets of imperatives is much more complex than this. There are strong echoes of the Ages Myth in the first set of imperatives: Justice and Oath recall Aidos and Nemesis (Justice like the guardians of the Golden

Age is cloaked in mist, 223 = 125); the fields are productive (ἔργα νέμονται 231 = ἔργ᾽ ἐνέμοντο 119); there are feasts (231 = 115); children are like their parents (235 vs. 182); the ζείδωρος ἄρουρα bears fruit (237 = 117, 173).[48]

In terms of audience expectation, the three stories have a very complex relationship with the three sets of imperatives. The first story offers both an aetiological explanation of the present (no *bios*; much disease) and a moral (Zeus cannot be fooled) and this creates the expectation of aetiology and moral for the other two. The second story, however, has only aetiology in its description of the Iron Age, although there seems to be the same moral as the first story implicit in it (Zeus will destroy the evil).[49] The fable has no aetiology, though the talk of a singer makes the allegorical force undeniable and we can easily supply an application (this is the Iron Age). The hawk gives us a moral (might makes right) but this is doubly unsatisfactory: it contradicts the moral of the two previous stories and formally it is within the fable rather than being a comment on the fable.[50] The moral we *want* to supply is that Zeus will destroy the evil but this wish is only gradually fulfilled, and it is not until the third set of imperatives that the need for commentary on the various stories is fully satisfied.[51]

The first step comes in the first set of imperatives: the hawk thinks he is one of the betters (κρείσσονας 210) but in fact it is the road to justice which is better (κρείσσων 217), a pointed echo since these are the only two occurrences of the word in the poem. The crying of the nightingale is recalled by Justice dragged through the streets bewailing the city but at the same time bringing evil to men (223f). The dynamics have changed: now the victim, the one wailing, can bring evil. Still it is unclear how Justice can be effective if she is being dragged along, and only in the second set of imperatives do we see her seated beside Zeus telling him about the unjust mind of men. We began with an example of animal *nomos* in the fable and this was followed by the first set of imperatives which told Perses to heed justice (ἄκουε Δίκης 213) because (γάρ 214) the just road is stronger (than the hawk) and Justice crying (like the nightingale) brings evil to men. Once Justice's power has been explained (her seat by Zeus reminds us of the τιμή given to Hecate's children) in the second set of imperatives, Hesiod again commands Perses to heed justice (Δίκης ἐπάκουε 275 = 213), explaining (γάρ 276 = 214) that Zeus has given man justice in contrast to the animals' *nomos* to eat each other. Schematically the pattern is: (a) animals eat each other—(b) Perses heed

Justice—(c) for Justice is stronger—(c) Justice sits by Zeus—(b) Perses heed Justice—(a) for it is better than animals eating each other.

The cumulative expectation for present application and moral, then, builds up until it is satisfied, ever more fully, by the three sets of imperatives. The first set rephrases the fable to make the hawk unjust and then describes the just and unjust cities, thereby answering both myths: it makes it clear that the woes of the Iron Age are the result of injustice and not just inevitable decline[52] and that the loss of *bios* in the Prometheus myth is not irrevocable (the implicit point of the Heroic Age). The dispenser of justice in both cities is Zeus and so the implicit moral is that of the Prometheus myth while the present application comes from both myths. The second set of imperatives is a totally negative set of threats from the 30,000 watchers, Justice and Zeus's eye, addressed to the kings, the details of which come from the Ages myth even though the moral is that of the Prometheus myth. Its main function is to reinforce, explain and justify the assertion that justice is κρείσσων. The third set, with its distinction between animal *nomos* and human justice, draws its conclusion from the second set and thereby gives the long-awaited answer to the fable which had challenged the limited optimism of the Ages myth and which was picked up by Hesiod's own wish, directly before the final set of imperatives, not to be just if injustice is rewarded.

This third and final answer to the question of justice fittingly ends the whole first part of the poem and it is introduced as was the whole part by a command to Perses to keep these things in mind (ὦ Πέρση, σὺ δὲ ταῦτα μετὰ φρεσὶ βάλλεο σῇσιν 274 = ὦ Πέρση, σὺ δὲ ταῦτα τεῷ ἐνικάθεο θυμῷ 27).[53] After being confused by the introduction of the kings at 202 and 248 when we expected only Perses (v.10), we turn back finally to Hesiod and Perses, with Zeus as guarantor of justice (273), recalling the end of the proem (9). The progress from 30,000 watchers to Zeus's daughter to Zeus's eye to Zeus himself is Hesiod's final answer to the kings.

Thus the two parts of the poem are thematically distinct and formally separated. The first part describes the world of bad Eris while the second exhorts us to follow the ways of good Eris. The audience, having heard the programmatic description of the two Erides, will expect a full description of both and so, when the three stories are answered by the three imperatives and we have begun once again to talk of seasonable livelihood and seizure of others' goods, we expect now to hear about good Eris, and this expectation is met by the

Almanac with its description of the farming of both seed and plant crops. The shift has been marked by a full address to Perses and talk of the easy road to poverty (κακότης) and the sweaty road to ἀρετή, i.e., social status and wealth as opposed to the good and evil of the first part.

The question remains why the Nautilia is not explicitly predicted in the program. Some critics have thought that it *is* predicted in 45f where we are told of the loss of the ideal life without agriculture or sailing, but this is not part of the program and only hindsight allows us to see this as a structurally significant statement.[54] In terms of audience expectation, West (45 n.2) is correct that there is "no hint that Hesiod plans to treat of sailing," and so the Nautilia is not really a separate part but only an extension of the Almanac, as is clear when we realize that it presumes sufficient *bios* for trade.[55] Not surprisingly, many critics join the two and speak of them as the "Calendar," as we have been doing. The Nautilia, then, is merely a footnote to the Almanac, an option in addition to agriculture that the wise man will choose either not at all or only during the summer. Hesiod ends the section with talk about breaking one's wagon (694), and so we return not to the beginning of the Nautilia but to the beginning of the Almanac.

A passage in the *Odyssey* may help explain the section's intent. Odysseus (disguised as a beggar!) says that he could talk for a year (εἰς ἐνιαυτόν) if only there were enough food and others to go to work (ἐπ' ἔργον, Od. 14.193–98). The phrase recalls Hesiod's admonition to Perses at the beginning of the poem (27ff) to avoid work (ἀπ' ἔργου) and take up court cases *only* when he has a year's livelihood (βίος ἐπηετανός). We may conclude that there are two different kinds of speech dependent on sufficient ἔργα, two different responses to sufficient livelihood, court λόγοι and Hesiod's singing λόγοι. In the Nautilia, on the other hand, Hesiod offers Perses a different option when he has sufficient *bios*—increase it in trade.[56] In a complementary way, Hesiod's own poetic activity (λιγυρῆς ἀοιδῆς 659) is an alternative to the summer relaxation listening to the piercing song (λιγυρὴν ἀοιδήν 583) of the cicada.

Formally the Nautilia is the negative afterimage of the Almanac. The two sections are balanced in a number of ways: both consider the whole year; both begin with conditionals setting the tone for the following imperatives (see West 253f); both have alternative times for their activities;[57] and both use the solstice for dating (663; 479, 564).

Sailing is what one should not do, at least most of the year when one is fully occupied with farming, and so Hesiod starts the section with the time to stop sailing (622). The advice he gives comes from one who has never sailed, except for a short trip to Euboia (650ff) and the only time he advises sailing is precisely the time he has earlier marked out for a bit of relaxation, the height of summer (θέρεος καματώδεος ὥρη 584 = θέρεος καματώδεος ὥρης 664).[58] The rich man will rest; the man who wishes to avoid poverty, like Hesiod's father, may turn to sailing.

We find a similar duplication in the myths, both of which seem to point to the same moral and describe the same polarities of present misery or past paradise. Hesiod points out the duplication when he introduces the Ages myth by saying, "if you wish I will sum up another story" (106). Not only is the Ages myth paired with the Prometheus myth as Nautilia is paired with Almanac but, as we will see in the following chapter, the unexpected parts of the myths, the mischievous Pandora and the Heroic Age, are echoed in the digressive, central portions of Almanac and Nautilia. Demonstration will require first an analysis of the two sections, Almanac and Nautilia, since the concept of a central section or of a digression is foreign to most readings of this part of the poem.

## Chapter Eight
## THE FORM OF THE CALENDAR

### A. *The Nautilia (618–94)*

The fullest formal analysis of this section is by Nicolai (125–27), who finds a three-part calendar (autumn 618–30; summer 663–77; spring 678–86) plus appendix (687–94) interrupted by a personal statement or "sphragis" (631–62), which is itself divided into two parts (Hesiod's father 631–40; Hesiod 648–62) with a transition in-between (641–47, rearranged). As Nicolai admits (125), this is hard to follow and in fact there is a much simpler, three-part structure once we realize that 631–40 is not part of the sphragis: sailing (618–45)—sphragis (646–62)—sailing (663–94).

The argument for not including the descriptions of Hesiod and his father in the same section is first that they are separated in the poem (thus Nicolai needs to rearrange lines to unite them). Also Hesiod begins the second section with a statement that parallels the first ("whenever you turn your mind to sailing" 645f = "if desire for sailing seizes you" 618). This is such a striking redundancy that West, following Lehrs, concluded that the lines "look very much like a slightly altered alternative opening to the sailing section."[1]

A final argument for separation is that the form of each section marks it off from the others. The first and third sections both have two long parts with contrasting sailing times followed by a short part discussing cargo:

(a)    618–29 bad time
(a¹)    630–40 good time
(b)    641–45 big cargo
(a¹)    663–77 good time
(a)    678–88 bad time
(b)    689–94 small cargo.

The sections begin with contrasting seasons ('do not sail in winter' 619ff vs. 'do sail in summer' 663ff) and end with contrasting talk about cargo : 'larger cargo (φόρτος) means larger profit' 644 vs. 'leave more at home, ship (φορτίζεσθαι) the lesser part' 690—words in φορτ- occur only here (631,643,644,672,690). Both sections talk about when sailing is ὡραῖος: 'wait for an ὡραῖον πλόον' 630 = 'now the πλόος is ὡραῖος' 665. The third section ends 'I bid you keep in mind all this as I tell you' (687f) while the first begins 'draw up your ship remembering to work the land as I bid you' (623f).[2] The central section, the sphragis, has its own order:

(a)  'I will show you the sea's measures' (648)
(b)  'even though I am not skilled in sailing or ships' (649f)
(c)  'although I did sail to Aulis' (651–659)
(b)  'that is the extent of my experience of ships' (660)
(a)  'but I will tell you Zeus's thought' (661).

The sphragis, then, is a self-contained, unified digressive whole.

Still one wants to know why Hesiod separated father and son as he did. The obvious answer is to contrast them: Hesiod does not sail but his father did (note the frequentative πλώζεσκ' 634)—he is, in Griffith's words (61), "the negative paradigm of a man who unwisely looked to the sea." To Hesiod's father Helikon is a terrible place (639f) while to Hesiod it is the home of his teachers, the Muses (688); Hesiod's father was poor while Hesiod won at least one prize. There also may be a contrast between the father's sons who have a legal dispute and the sons of Amphidamas who unite to offer the prizes for their father.[3] In the first part, the absence of *bios* meant the necessity for work and avoiding the courts while the presence of *bios* allowed attendance at court. Here the absence of *bios* has caused Hesiod's father to sail and, judging from *Odyssey* 14.193ff, we may assume it is the presence of *bios* that allows Hesiod to sing. Perses is no singer and Hesiod may be suggesting that given sufficient *bios* he is better off sailing than attending court.

The closer contrast, however, is between Hesiod and the Greek heroes of the Trojan war who were mentioned in the Heroic Age, and it is this contrast, I think, that justifies the centrality of the digressive sphragis. The Greeks travelled to war and their prize was a woman (so Troy is καλλιγύναικα 653);[4] Hesiod travelled to a contest and his prize was an eared tripod (657). They travelled a long distance by sea and had to wait out a winter storm; Hesiod travelled a short distance ("perhaps 100 yards" Griffin 95) and would never sail during the winter (χειμῶνα 652 = χειμῶν' 675). Also the description of the Heroic Age emphasizes the distance over sea the Greeks had to travel (ὑπὲρ μέγα λαῖτμα θαλάσσης 164), and the Nautilia is almost the only other place in the poem that θάλασσα is mentioned.[5] The contrast is heightened by the fact that Troy and the Trojan War are mentioned only here and in the description of the Heroic Age (653, 165).[6]

The next question is why the Heroic Age is singled out for comparison. The Gold and Silver Ages are divine (δαίμονες, 122 μάκαρες 141) and therefore different in kind from the following races (thus the Silver Age is rewarded after death despite its lack of virtues).[7] The Bronze Age has become anonymous (νώνυμοι 154) and so cannot be spoken of. Furthermore, the Heroic Age is the one preceding the present and Hesiod said he would rather have lived in the preceding one or be born in the next one.[8] More important, I think, is the fact that the Heroic Age breaks the downward slide of the Ages, is juster and better, a godlike (θεῖον 159) race.[9] The farmer may struggle to accomplish a life far worse than the Golden or Silver Age, whose joys are accessible only to the truly just city, but Hesiod has done much better than the Heroic Age, replacing war with poetic competition and avoiding winter sailing.[10] The Greeks sailed to war but Hesiod sailed to a poetic competition, a war of words not deeds; they sailed during winter,[11] a time Hesiod says one should not sail, while he with this one exception does not sail at all.

As the Heroic Age has reversed the downward trend of the metallic Ages, so Hesiod himself reverses the predicted final plunge of the Iron Age and sets the model for Perses. He knows reverence toward the gods as the Iron Age would not (θεῶν ὄπιν 187) for he dedicates his prize to the Muses who taught him his song and encourages reverence in others (ὄπιν ἀθανάτων 706). Also he is a friendly brother who wants to dissolve the strife his unfriendly brother has started and will shortly recommend that one have a brother as his best friend (707) whereas the sign of the end of the Iron Age will be when brother is no longer a friend as before (184). Hesiod does not use words to blame as the people at the end of the Iron Age will (186) but to instruct (or to compete)—rather it is Perses who is using words badly, either in court or begging. Whereas the Iron Age is in danger of losing all contact with the gods at the departure of Aidos and Nemesis (200), Hesiod is close to Zeus, whose spokesman he is, thanks to the Muses (661f).

One final point. The relationship between Hesiod and Zeus recalls the prologue, where Zeus was to assure justice and Hesiod would speak to Perses, but here the split between the two has been effaced as Hesiod is able to speak the thought (νόον) of Zeus (661). This is quite an advance over 483f, where the thought (νόος) of Zeus was difficult for men to understand. One might even say that Helikon (658) has replaced Pieria (1) as the home of the Muses. The possibility of such an allusion is strengthened by v.659 which has seemed to many critics a direct reference to the investiture described in the *Theogony*. Hesiod will then be contrasting the *Works and Days* which promotes good Eris (e.g. the poetic contest) with the *Theogony* which promotes bad Eris (e.g. the Trojan War).[12]

## B. The Almanac (383–617)

The form of the Almanac is much less orderly than that of the Nautilia although it is generally agreed that there are three major sections, broadly defined by seasons: fall (383–492), winter (493–563), spring (564–617).[13] Nicolai (89f) notes that such a scheme, with three seasons rather than four and with its beginning in fall rather than spring is not the obvious one and rightly concludes that fall and spring represent the thematic poles of sowing and reaping, with winter as an insert (Einlage).

One thing that marks Winter off from the preceding section is its beginning. The picture of a talker who lacks *bios* (493ff) recalls the description of Hesiod's legal dispute that opens the first part, where Perses was told to avoid being a listener at the agora (29) since the man lacking *bios* (31) has little time for disputes or talk. The opening of the Almanac likewise begins with a talker lacking *bios*: the needy Perses (ἀχρεῖος . . . χρειῶν 403f) is told to work and not to beg, seeking food (βίοτον 400) and speaking useless words (ἐτώσια . . . ἀγορεύσεις 402). The ἐτωσιοεργός talker does not fill his basket (καλιήν 411).[14] Like these two earlier beginnings, the beginning of the Winter section presents us with another talker who lacks *bios* and who, like the ἐτωσιοεργός talker of 411, lacks καλιάς (503):[15]

> (a) the seat at the smithy (χαλκεῖον θῶκον 493) must be avoided,[16] and work must be done, for the unworking man (ἀεργὸς ἀνήρ 498),
> (b) waiting for empty hope and needing food (χρήιζων βιότοιο 499),
> (c) speaks evil in his heart;
> (b) hope is not good for the man in need (500),
> (a) seated in the hall, if he does not have *bios* (501).

The main contrast that the Winter section offers to the other parts of the Almanac is in its content: "a succession of highly poetic pictures" (West 54) with very little in the way of work to be done.[17] Also there is a chronological displacement since before the Winter section begins we jump ahead to spring plowing (462).[18] Further there is a general contrast with the other seasons: man is helpless, dependent, without work. There are a number of specific contrasts as well: the equinox seems to be alluded to in the talk of nights and days being equal (562), while solstices are used as dates in both fall and spring (479, 564); the winter month Lenaion is called "ox-flaying" (504)[19] while in fall one is told to get an ox (405); the sun is absent in winter (526) but very much present in fall and spring (e.g. 414, 479, 612); in winter there is vital need for clothes (536ff) but one must strip to sow (in fall) and to reap (in spring, 391f);[20] winter has a named month (504) whereas the other seasons have dating by birds and stars; in the Winter section people are described in terms of manufactured objects (wheel 518, tripod 533) while in fall people manufacture wagon and plow (423ff); in winter one should avoid the smithy (493) while other times the smithy is useful for making a plow (430); in winter we find a delicate παρθένος inside (519f) while in fall the hired or slave γυνή works outside (405f). Perhaps in some sense winter represents society, with its focus on the smithy, its mention of the παρθένος (527) and its named month as opposed to natural dating.

Not only does winter stand alone and offer a strong contrast to fall, but the Spring section that follows recalls fall in a number of details and represents the end-point outlined at the beginning of the Almanac. The Almanac begins with the Pleiades as the key sign for both reaping and plowing (384) and, as we hear about plowing soon thereafter (450ff), so we expect reaping.[21] That is what we get in the Spring section (575ff), and the chiastic order (reaping, plowing, plowing, reaping) reinforces the connection. The Almanac ends by again mentioning plowing and the Pleiades (615f) thereby returning us to its beginning.[22] Likewise, the Almanac begins with the extended description of the cutting the wood for a wagon (423ff), but the wagon will be used only to harvest the crop, which is described in the Spring section. Particular echoes of the Fall section in the Spring section include: bird songs (swallow 568 cf. crane 448, cuckoo 486), mention of the solstices (564 cf. 479), the ox, the hired hand, getting a childless woman and a dog (602ff) which recall the injunction to get a house, a woman and a plow ox (405).

Scholars, then, are correct to see the Winter section as the central part of the Almanac,[23] and here too, as in the center of the Nautilia, we find a strong echo of the mythic first part. The focus of the description of Lenaion at the center of the Winter section is the maiden, who is warm inside while those outside are cold, and is naked while those outside are clothed and by whom water is desired rather than avoided.[24] This maiden is the most obvious echo of the Pandora story. Unlike Pandora she is a παρθένος not a mixture of παρθένος and γυνή (cf. 63, 71 vs. 80, 94); she knows nothing of Aphrodite (521) while Pandora was decked out by Aphrodite (65). The lazy man who will stop at the smithy and chat, depending on ἐλπίς rather than work (498, 500), reminds us of Pandora's deceptive gift to man (96). We may even be permitted to see in the implicit emphasis on fire in the descriptions of both the smithy and the maiden washing a reflection of Prometheus' theft of fire (especially since the maiden is contrasted to the octopus with his fireless home, 525). Woman has now become innocent and safe and fire has become helpful: the phrase describing the maiden remaining inside the house (δόμων ἔντοσθε . . . μίμνει 520; cf. 523) recalls the contents of the pithos which, before Pandora let them out, remained inside in their unbreakable house (ἐν ἀρρήκτοισι δόμοισιν / ἔνδον ἔμιμνε 96f).[25] It is important to note that what is echoed is not the core of the Prometheus story (Mekone, theft of fire, dressing the goddess) but the addition to it made in the *Works and Days*: the pithos, maiden and hope.

Thus we see that at the center of the two main sections of Calendar, Almanac and Nautilia, lie modern individuals (the generalized winter woman; the particular Hesiod) who are strongly reminiscent of the focal points of the two myths of the first part (the particular Pandora and her pithos; the generalized Heroic Age). In both myths the focal points are also changes or additions to the expected story. In both sets of echoes the depressing moral outlined in the first part has been at least partially overturned, and so beyond the simple structural function of binding each myth with a part of the Calendar these echoes have a particular meaning: good Eris will replace bad; as the poet can recover the Golden Age, so women can be redeemed from the curse of Pandora and we can return from the Iron Age perhaps to something even better than the Heroic.

The final and most surprising strand in this web of interconnections involves the two central digressions of the Calendar, which are bound together by both image and theme. The most obvious echoes are the recurrence of the sea (εὑρέι πόντῳ 507 = εὑρέα πόντον 650) during a winter storm (524, 652) and the tripod (533, 657). Since these are the only tripods in the poem, calling the tripod "eared" in

657 may be meant to recall the human tripod of 533 and not be just a standard epithet. Also, here alone are the Greeks mentioned by name (528, 653), and talk is located in the center of this section as well as the other.[26] More generally there is a contrast between the παρθένος who knows nothing of Aphrodite, kept safe inside and Troy with its beautiful woman (καλλιγύναικα 653) Helen, who we know was Aphrodite's prize to Paris.

We have seen a complex interconnection between the "heavy parts," to use West's term, of each half of the poem: the Ages myth balances the Prometheus/Pandora myth as Nautilia balances Almanac. Further, the unexpected parts of the myths, the mischievous Pandora and the Heroic Age, are echoed in the digressive, central portions of Almanac and Nautilia, which in turn share both images and themes.

## C. Form of the Second Part

We saw earlier that the "heavy parts" of the first section were integrated into a complex whole in which the two myths and the fable were answered by three sets of imperatives. The second part, too, is carefully articulated, and once again the audience has its suspended expectations finally realized. As we have seen, the introduction to the second part clearly echoes the introduction to the first part. After this close echo, we have a "free-wheeling" (West 45) set of disparate injunctions (335–80) that must have confused the early Greek audiences as much as it confuses modern critics.[27] The pattern is discernible only after the Nautilia when we have a similar set of injunctions (695–764). These two sets of injunctions which surround the Calendar, as has long been recognized, share content as well as form.[28] One can go a step further, I think, and argue that they seem to show a development, so that the second set in several cases reverses the injunctions of the first. In a sense, then, they mark the movement of the Calendar from the despair of the Iron Age.[29] In addition, the focus has narrowed from the individual in relationship to other individuals to the individual by himself.

The two sets of injunctions are unified in their break from their surroundings and parallel in form (infinitive for imperative) and content. There is also a noticeable difference in tone from what precedes: in the 46 lines of the first set of injunctions (335–380) there are as many commands as there are in the preceding 334 lines.[30] This sets the tone for the basically imperatival second part of the poem. Still the precise limits are not easy to define.

Of the two, the series after the Almanac is easier to delimit despite the use of imperatival infinitives in the preceding section since except for the possibly transitional 694 the material that precedes is about sailing and what follows is not. The section ends with a return to regular imperatives and a cluster of gnomai about φήμη described in terms that seem to many critics to recall the very beginning of the poem: ῥεῖα 762 recalls ῥεῖα 5,6,7; 'evil' fame is substantially like 'blameworthy' Eris and both are cases of divine personification. Also, the danger of bad reputation is the converse of the proem's statement that Zeus makes the haughty unspoken of (ἄφατοι 3, ἄρρητοι4).[31] What follows is a clearly different section, the Days. So, the second set of injunctions comprises 695–764.

The first set of injunctions is harder to delimit. It clearly ends at 380 if we consider 381f transitional (following Nicolai 87), but different scholars begin it at quite different places: at 342 (Steitz 166, Benardete 150, Nicolai 72, Mazon [1928] 75, van Groningen 286, Aly 30, Schmidt 55), at 335 (Fuss 61f, Kerschensteiner 185, La Penna *apud* Verdenius 170, Schwabl [1970] 466, Bona Quaglia 194), at 327 (Wilamowitz 132, Blusch 134, Schmid 273, Solmsen [1982] 10 n.30, Thalmann 57, Barron 99), at 320 (West 45) or at 286 (Diller 48, Heath 246).

The addresses to Perses provide one clue. Perses is addresssd or mentioned by name at structurally key points throughout the first part of the poem: end of invocation (10), end of program (27), introducing the sets of imperatives after the myth (213, 274) and twice at the beginning of the second part (286, 299).[32] He is not addressed again until 397 and then at the end of the Almanac (611) and to articulate the Nautilia (633, 641). From this we can conclude that the break is somewhere between the addresses at 299 and 397, but the use of the second singular throughout the section (306, 312, 316, 335, 341, 350f, 361f, 367, 373) makes further precision impossible on formal grounds. Content is a better guide: as we have seen, echoes of the introduction to the poem's first part extend to 326 and so the break must come after that. Since the imperatival infinitives begin at 336 (so already Steitz 106), symmetry with the later set of injunctions suggests the invocation at 335 as the dividing point (ἀλλὰ σὺ δέ . . .).[33] We will see that the balance between the two sets of injunctions is formally very close, but we must remember that the listening audience would have no such means of deciding.

If we look at the actual injunctions in the two sections, we find that the first section looks to the Prometheus/Pandora myth and Hesiod's legal dispute in arguing (a) that one cannot trust a brother (371), as Epimetheus and Perses have both shown; (b) that neighbors are better helpers than one's relatives (345);[34] and finally (c) that one should pray for only a single child (376), thereby avoiding dividing the food (and the inheritance).[35] One should sacrifice to the gods so they will have a propitious heart (340), as opposed to Zeus who was angered (at the thwarted sacrifice, 47).[36] So much for brothers and gods; the third member of Prometheus' acquaintances, Pandora, is met in the 'smart-assed woman' who deceives (373)[37] and wants to steal one's basket, as Pandora tampered with the storage pithos. Her wily words (374) are almost a direct echo of Pandora (78),[38] and Pandora's thievish nature (67) is echoed when Hesiod says "who trusts a woman, trusts thieves" (375).[39]

The second set of injunctions reverses the negative evaluation of brother and wife. We begin with advice on picking a wife, who should be a παρθένος (699, recalling the παρθένος of winter vs. Pandora) and a neighbor (700), thereby equating neighbors and relatives, whereas before they were opposed. Finally she should not be a food-ambusher (δειπνολόχης 704), a phrase which reminds us of the smart-assed basket-seeking woman we met earlier (374), for such a one will parch a man without a torch (705). The mention of parching (εὔει) may be meant to recall the drying effect of summer ("the skin dries up from the heat" 588), a time when the women are most wanton and the men weakest.[40] After a line about reverence to the gods that reverses the Iron Age sacrilege (706, excised by many critics), we hear that one should not make a friend the equal of a brother. Thus brother/relative and wife/woman have been recovered from the extremely negative valuation of the first part of the poem, much as bad Eris has been replaced by good Eris.[41] Finally, the only mention of δίκη in the second part of the poem occurs here: after saying not to make a friend the equal of a brother, Hesiod goes on to say that, if you do, do not wrong him first but, if he wrongs you, pay him back double but accept it if he wishes to become a friend again and offers δίκη (707–13). One might easily see the relationship between Hesiod and Perses summarized here.

It may seem that this long list of negative imperatives is less op-

timistic than the earlier positive set, but we should note that the pro-
hibitions are all easily controlled by the individual. Also, a list of negative commands can be considered more optimistic than a list of
positive commands since the former allows virtually unlimited free-
dom. Instead of sacrificing to the gods day and night (338f), one need
only beware of easily-avoided ritually incorrect actions: wash your
hands before a libation (724f), do not urinate facing the sun (727) or
naked at night (730), do not cut your nails at a feast (742f).

The second set of injunctions reverses the first in structure as
well as content. The first set begins with

> (a) the need for sacrifices done properly (ἀγνῶς καὶ καθαρῶς
> 336–4l) and then considers
> (b) whom one should invite to the feast (342–48) and finally
> moves to
> (c) an extended discussion of give and take among friends and
> neighbors (349–78).

The second set of injunctions begins with

> (c) the reversal of the earlier judgment on wives, brothers and
> neighbors (695–714) through
> (b) the proper attitude toward feasts (715, 722f) and finally
> (a) the proper behavior toward the gods, first in terms of man
> himself (724–41), then man and external objects (beginning with the
> feast 742–45).[42]

The return to the gods clearly prepares us for the Days that follow,
but also implies that societal norms have now been reestablished by
the Calendar so that one can move to the more private religious
norms. The focus has shifted in this second set from the larger society
to the individual and his οἶκος. Earlier it was a matter of inviting a
friend to a feast; now one must think about how to position the ladle
on the winebowl. Earlier the focus was on how to treat one's family,
friends and neighbors; now it is how to treat one's own body. Earlier
it was a matter of doing things to or for others; now it is for oneself.

We may conclude, then, that the poem divides into two parts,
each internally articulated and prepared by the twofold program outlined directly following the hymnic invocation. The first part begins
with a description of the legal dispute between Hesiod and Perses and
then gives three stories, two myths and a fable, which are answered
in order by three sets of imperatives. The second part likewise begins
with a scene between Hesiod and Perses (now Perses is a beggar) fol-

lowed by a long set of injunctions that is answered by a parallel set after the Calendar. The central units of the first part, the two myths, have two digressive sections, the pithos story and the Heroic Age, and these two sections are echoed in the central, digressive sections of the two main units of the second part, the description of winter in the Almanac and of Hesiod's poetic victory in the Nautilia. Finally, these two central sections are themselves connected in image and theme. West's assumption that the poem could stop anywhere is refuted by the presence of the program, which demands that good Eris be treated in the same depth as bad Eris. His complaint about the lack of logic and beauty and Edwards' assumption that the poem has no structure are refuted by the subtle but noticeable series of echoes articulating the main parts.

More than any other section of the poem, the so-called Days (765–828) has been the object of scholarly dispute. It is not only un-predicted by the program but also at first appears internally incoher-ent, self-contradictory and totally incidental to the rest of the poem.[1] Since we find probable additions embedded in the manuscript tradi-tion of the *Theogony*, we might easily conclude that the Days is simi-larly intrusive. Also, a number of critics have noted that 760–64 would make a fitting end to the whole poem and so conclude that the Days are added.[2]

The main problem is the incoherence of the section itself: we begin with the end of the month and then proceed through the month with the first, fourth, seventh, eighth, ninth, eleventh, twelfth, thirteenth and sixteenth but then back to the sixth, the eighth and twelfth before going on to the twentieth, then back again to the tenth and fourteenth, back further to the fourth, the fifths (i.e., fifth, fifteenth and twenty-fifth), then to the seventeenth and nineteenth but then back to ninth, fourth, fourteenth and twenty-fourth. An-other problem is that the list ends with the statement that "these days are a great benefit for mortals" (822) even though many of the days have something bad about them and some days (the fifths) are to be avoided entirely. Finally, the section seems out of harmony with the earlier part of the poem in its "superstitious" tone and in some of its particular injunctions for, as Solmsen has noted, the farmer told to set sail fifty days after the summer solstice (663) and on the "thrice-ninth" day (814) will generally not be able to satisfy both recommen-dations.[3]

Critics who have not discarded the whole section have offered two interpretations of its form. The usual response is to isolate a He-siodic core and then argue that the rest is a series of accretions, often contradictory in nature. This position has been argued recently by Solmsen (1963; accepted by Samuel, Heath 252), who is willing to grant at most 769–779 (the "original stock" 298) to Hesiod; Jimenez, who excises only 810–21, and Roesch, who credits Hesiod with the farming advice contained in the forward-numbered days.[4] At the other extreme are the "associative" critics who argue that the basic form has been complicated by chains of ideas connected to each other by key words or phrases. Verdenius was the first to discuss this in detail regarding the Days and he has been followed by West (58), who argues that although the outline is basically the month from beginning to end it has been expanded by associative "departures" (58). Yet he allows more departures (seven) than days in order (six) and so his structure has little fixity to it. Both of these interpretative methods have in common the assumption of a basic plan plus other material that does not fit.

A mistake fundamental to all interpretations has been lack of attention to the rhetoric of the section. Hesiod begins by saying that one should guard well the "days from Zeus" (ἤματα δ' ἐκ Διόθεν πεφυλαγμένος εὖ κατὰ μοῖραν 765) and then goes on to describe appropriate activities for the thirtieth, ending "for the following are the Days from thoughtful Zeus" (αἵδε γὰρ ἡμέραι εἰσὶ Διὸς παρὰ μητιόεντος 769). He then lists five days: the "old," the fourth, the seventh (a "holy day") , the eighth and the ninth (770–72a).[5] Critics have always assumed that *all* the days mentioned in 765–828 are "days from Zeus" but this seems unlikely for several reasons. First the days after 772a are separated grammatically and thematically from the list in 770–72a: "two days are outstanding for mortal works (βροτήσια ἔργα) the eleventh and the twelfth (772b–74)."[6] This is not only a new sentence and a discrete list ("two days") but also, unlike the previous list, it goes on to describe both what one should do on these days (shear sheep, gather crops) and why one day is better than the other. The "days from Zeus," on the other hand, have no activity attached to them and no difference made between them, except that the seventh is holy because it is Apollo's birthday (which does not mean that it is better than the other "days from Zeus"). Finally there is an implicit contrast between the divine days from Zeus (one even labelled "holy") and the days good for mortals (βροτήσια ἔργα).

Given the focus on the six days "from Zeus," the audience will inevitably want to know what activities are to be associated with them. Hesiod does not tell us this immediately and one must wait until the second half of the section to hear much about any one of them (except the eighth, on which it is good to castrate boar and ox, 790, and the middle fourth, which is good for a girl to be born, 794). After 797, however, we hear in detail about many of the days: the middle seventh, for example, is good not only for winnowing but also wood-cutting; the "thrice-ninth" is good for beginning the pithos, yoking oxen, mules and horses, and launching a ship. Equally striking, we hear *only* about these days (except for the fifths, which are to be avoided) and we hear about them in fairly good order: first and last fourth (798–801),[7] the avoided fifths (802–4), the middle seventh (805–8, with the fourth mentioned again 809), the middle and first ninths (810–13) and then the mystifying "thrice-ninth"(814–18)[8] and then we end with a reprise of all the fourths, first, middle and "after-twentieth" (819–21).[9] Revealingly, all we hear about the middle fourth is that it is a "holy day" (ἱερὸν ἦμαρ) precisely the same phrase, found in the same metrical position, as the description of the seventh in the original listing of the "days from Zeus" (819 = 770). The apparent exception, the bad fifths, is really suited only to this section since it, like the "holy" seventh, is the birthday of a god. Since that god is the child of the bad Eris that man is to avoid, the fifths too must be avoided by man, although they are equally holy. We seem to have here a reflection of the contrast between good and bad Eris.

There is, then, a basic split at 797, and one can contrast the clear order of the second half with the chaotic order of the first, whose main section (780–97) seems to be organized more by content than chronology (especially days good or bad for children: ἀνδρογόνος . . . κούρη δ' 783, κούρη 785, ἀνδρογόνος 788, ἀνδρογόνος . . . κούρη δέ 794). The contrast between the two halves involves content as well: the second half gives us the concerns of the rest of the poem, plowing, threshing, ships, pithoi, marriage, as well as specifying the first ninth as a day good for planting or bearing a child, male or female. The first half, once we are past the two days good for mortal works (772–79), talks almost exclusively about days that are good or bad for bearing children or gelding and taming animals. Not only are the days of the first half bad for animal reproduction and very ambivalent for either male or female children (as opposed to the wholly good ninth in the second half), but they are days only of birth (ἀνδρογόνος 783, 788, 794; γενέσθαι 784, γείνασθαι 793), over which one has no control, rather than "planting" (φυτευέμεν 812) over which one does have control. To the extent that the first half is concerned with work, it is the work more of the shepherd than the farmer; 780f confirms this for it says to avoid planting seed on the thirteenth.[10] We are reminded of the differing nature of the Winter section, with its concern for hides, weaving, clothes-making and the relative insulation of cattle, goats and sheep.

Structural considerations confirm the division. Both parts begin with the same injunction to guard the days: πεφύλαξο 797 echoes πεφυλαγμένος 765 and both close with mention of fourth and twentieth (εἰκάδι . . . τετρὰς μέσση 792–5 ~ τετράδι . . . μέσση . . . μετεικάδα 819–20). The second part is further articulated by its description of shipping: cutting timber on the middle seventh (808), then beginning building on the fourth (809) and finally launching on the "thrice-ninth" (817f). Also the second part is ringed by mention of judging birds: οἰωνοὺς κρίνας 801 ~ ὄρνιθας κρίνων 828; and we should remember that birds were a repeated chronological marker in the Calendar. Finally, one should note that the second half repeatedly stresses beginnings (809, 815), opening the pithos (819) and dawn (821 cf. 810). The whole section of the Days, then, begins at the end, the thirtieth, and ends with the beginning, the fourths, and with dawn.

We are now in a position to address the problem of 822, where the days are called "a great benefit for mortals." First we should note that the days are specified as "these days" (αἵδε μὲν ἡμέραι 822) which recalls in meter as well as phrasing the specification of "these (following) days" in the list of days from Zeus (αἵδε γὰρ ἡμέραι 769). Not surprisingly, the two sets of days are the same: we begin with a list of days from Zeus that comprises the "old", the fourth, the seventh, the eighth and the ninth. The second part, which for the most part describes these days, ends with the same phrase, "these days." Thus the days that are a great benefit for mortals are Zeus's days and only Zeus's days. The statement, then, is true: Zeus's days are beneficial, in contrast to the mass of ambiguous days described in 780–97.

The contrast between the two parts of the Days has several purposes. We have already seen that the birth of Eris's child may reflect the contrast between good and bad Eris basic to the form of the whole poem and that the focus on animals in the first part is earlier found only in the Winter section of the Calendar. More obviously, the contrast between the two sections in terms of marriage and birth reflects the contrast between the two sets of injunctions and repeats the movement from unfavorable to favorable evaluation of women, marriage and sex that we find has developed in a fairly coherent fashion through the poem. Hesiod's first and most important story to Perses concerns Pandora and her pithos, a παρθένος γυνή, a woman (wife?) who resembles (but is not) a "modest maiden" (71), and two brothers, one intelligent (Prometheus/Hesiod) and one foolish (Epimetheus/ Perses).

If we look—as we must to avoid the charge of subjectivity—at all the occurrences of marriage, woman, maiden, brother and jar in the poem, we see a clear and consistent reclamation of woman from the nadir Pandora embodies.[11] First the Pandora situation is recapitulated in the series of injunctions preceding the Calendar: "don't trust your brother; beware of the alluringly decked-out γυνή who will flatter you, seeking after your storage bin (371–75).[12] The mention of storage bin recalls Pandora's jar; and, not surprisingly, this is preceded by an injunction involving a jar.[13] The Calendar, however, begins with the recognition that there is some value in woman: Hesiod says that one must obtain, along with house, cow and plow, a woman to follow the cattle, but she should be a slave not a wife (405f).[14] Next we find παρθένος contrasted with γυνή as part of a general contrast of winter—where a sunny seat is good (493); Boreas' winds are bad (506ff); work is necessary (495); meals are reduced almost by half (559); the maiden inside, washing herself (an image of purity) is safe (519–21)—and summer, where Zephyr's breeze is good (594); a seat in the sun is bad (587, 593); instead of work one may feast to satiety (593); women are most lascivious and men dried up (586). The contrast leads to the marriage injunctions at the end of the Calendar, where one must marry a protected παρθένος whom one can teach and must avoid a bad γυνή who "singes without a torch" (705, recalling summer's dried up man) and "ambushes your dinner" (704, recalling the sought-after storage bin). The possibility of a good woman has now led to a total reversal of the earlier injunctions: thus, "marry when you're thirty; marry a παρθένος, make sure she is a good woman and a neighbor" (695–701) and "don't make a friend the equal of a brother" (707).

The movement from an unfavorable to a favorable view of women, marriage and sex is repeated in the Days. In the first half (780–97) we hear first of days that are good for producing men (783, 788, 794) but bad for women to be born (784, 785) or to marry (784).[15] In the second half, by contrast, we hear of a day good for marriage (ἄγεσθ᾽ εἰς οἶκον ἄκοιτιν 800 echoes γυναῖκα τεὸν ποτὶ οἶκον ἄγεσθαι 695) and then one good for either a male or female to be born or to give birth (812).[16] The last task mentioned is the opening of the pithos (819), and when we remember that the unfavorable view of woman began with Pandora, who opened the pithos and let out all the evils of the world, we can appreciate the rehabilitation that has been accomplished.

As for the foolish brother, he too has been rehabilitated by the time we reach the Days. We began with Epimetheus, whose trouble was that he did not listen to his brother Prometheus: οὐδ' Ἐπιμηθεύς / ἐφράσαθ' ὥς οἱ ἔειπε Προμηθεύς (85f). Throughout the Calendar Hesiod has been telling Perses to pay heed (φράζεσθαι 404, 448) and follow his advice (ὥς σε κελεύω 316, 536, 623) while his last personal command in the Calendar directly recalls Epimetheus: σ' ἄνωγα / φράζεσθαι τάδε πάντα μετὰ φρέσιν, ὡς ἀγορεύω (687). The Calendar opens with three types: the πανάριστος who, like Zeus, understands everything (πάντα νοήσει 293 = πάντα νοήσας 267); the ἐσθλός who obeys one speaking well (εὖ εἰπόντι 295) and finally the ἀχρήιος who neither understands nor heeds. Hesiod is the πανάριστος—his implicit relationship with Zeus becomes explicit in the Nautilia where he is able to speak the mind of Zeus (Ζηνὸς νόον 661)—and Perses has the choice of listening to his wiser brother (ἐσθλός 295 recalls Hesiod advising ἐσθλά in 286), who speaks well (εὖ εἰπόντι 295 recalls Hesiod narrating the Ages myth εὖ καὶ ἐπισταμένως 107), or continuing to be ἀχρήιος (cf. ἀχρεῖος δ' ἔσται ἐπέων νομός 403). Despite Hesiod's repeated injunctions there seems to have been no progress during the Calendar: Perses is still as foolish at the end (νήπιος 633) as he was at its beginning (286, 297). The Days, however, marks a striking reversal not only of Perses' attitude but of the whole situation between the brothers. It opens with Perses advising his servants rather than Hesiod giving him advice[17] and the advice he is to give is to oversee (ἐποπτεύειν) the work (ἔργα 767 = fields?) and to divide up the produce—reversing Hesiod's earlier advice to Perses *not* to look on at strife (ὀπιπεύοντ' 29) and to avoid further dividing their property. Now we have the people (λαοί) judging truth (768) rather than corrupt kings falsely judging Hesiod's case. Now it is the days which are a μέγ' ὄνειαρ (822) whereas before it was just mallow and asphodel (41).[18] At the very end we find the knowledgeable individual (τάδε πάντα / εἰδώς 826f) who obtains happiness by judging birds and avoiding ὑπερβασίας (828), particularly appropriate when one remembers how often bird signs have articulated the Almanac (crane 448, cuckoo 486, swallow 568). Even if Perses is not yet the πανάριστος who knows everything, still he has a limited body of knowledge (τάδε recalls ταῦτα 27, 274, beginning and ending the first part) which, if he can master all of it, will make him happy and blessed.[19]

The sense of a new beginning is confirmed in a number of ways at the very end: the pithos will be opened (815, 819), the oxen will be yoked (816), ships launched (817) and dawn will be best (821). We should note also how the Days begins at the end, with reaping and shearing (775), just as it begins with the 30th (766), the end of the month.[20] Between these endings and the beginnings at the end comes preparation: making children, gelding animals, making boats. Thematically we return to beginnings too: Pandora's destructive emptying of the pithos has now been reversed. In the first set of injunctions we heard that one should not be sparing at beginning and end of the pithos but only middle (368) and now we go back even further to the opening of a pithos, which is peaceful and helpful (815, 819). These are the only times the pithos is mentioned in the poem. Furthermore the paradox of Pandora's "bitchy" mind and thievish nature (67), echoed in the thievish woman seeking the basket (373f), is finally resolved when the farmer is told to get(?) a dog to guard against thieves (604f), and this resolution is taken back one final step in the Days where that κύνα καρχαρόδοντα (796 = 604) is first tamed.

Chronologically, as critics have noted, the Days forms the logical end point: we began with Ages, moved to the calendar year and now end with the month.[21] Within the month we move from days to parts of days (810, 821). Now that we understand the order of the Days we can see that Hesiod has here again, as in the Almanac, taken a simple chronological order and played with it and that his playing has a purpose. Furthermore, we should note that in both sections the space devoted to actual advice is hardly more than that given to the chronological points.[22] In fact, Hesiod spends more time describing temporal markers in the Almanac than he does telling how to plow, sow, reap and thresh. The ideal, outlined before the Prometheus myth, would be for a day to equal a year (43f) and here with the month recapitulating the year we have come at least part way. A similar pattern marks the development of man, beginning with the creation of (wo)mankind in the Prometheus myth (clearer in the *Theogony* version), moving to the evolution of different races in the Ages myth ending with the city structure of the Iron Age (189) and then from the city structure of the just and unjust cities (222, 227, 240, 269) to the household in the Calendar [23] and the individual in the injunctions preceding the Days and in the Days itself.

## Chapter Ten
## CONCLUSION

Before summing up, we need to address a fundamental problem. The analysis has been based to a large extent on repeated words and phrases and there is danger of subjectivity in this procedure. In the first place a repetition may suggest either comparison or contrast; secondly there are a number of comparisons/contrasts into which it can fit; finally, there may be other repetitions that are ignored because they do not fit.[1] We have seen that in almost every case contrast rather than comparison is suggested—not surprising in a poet many have found "antithetical"[2]—and I have tried to guard against arbitrary discrimination by including all examples of a word in my analysis and by looking for clusters of repetitions which individually may be random but in a group are less likely to be so. The third danger is one that has not been addressed and so it may be fitting to end this study with a quick test.

If we take a list of all repeated phrases in the poem, we can easily test the effectiveness of the model by seeing how many repetitions fit and how many do not. Krafft's lists of formulae in Hesiod provides a convenient, accessible and recent body of data.[3] He lists over ninety repetitions in the *Works and Days* (and about twice as many in the *Theogony*). Twenty-seven of these should be excluded as non-distinctive, either because their basic words are repeated frequently (in or outside one or more formulae) or because they have too little content.[4] Six occur in such close proximity that they are probably simply verbal reflexes. Of the remaining forty-five, forty-three have been or can be explained by the present study.

One remains which has no obvious structural function:

#241 εὐτροχάλῳ ἐν ἀλωῇ (599, 806)

One argues *against* the present analysis: #944 τῷ δὲ θεοὶ νεμεσῶσι (303, 741) suggests that the first set of injunctions should be extended back before 336 if it is to parallel the second set.

This simple test is reassuring, although we should realize that Krafft generally singles out only phrases repeated in the same metrical position while this study presupposes that repetition anywhere in the line is significant.

The essential conclusion of this inquiry is that the *Works and Days* has two antithetical parts, defined by the program describing the two Erides (11–26) and supported by the formal closure at 286 created by the three stories and their three matching sets of imperatives and by the gradual resolution of the moral problem implicit in the description of the Iron Age and graphically presented in the fable. 287ff is marked as a new beginning by the striking address to Perses immediately preceding the description of the ways to κακότης (poverty) or ἀρετή (wealth and social status), by the cluster of echoes from the beginning of the first part and by the second encounter of Hesiod and his brother, now a beggar, to match the first encounter over the legal dispute. In addition to these formal links, there are a number of thematic oppositions that occur throughout the poem. Zeus the god of justice becomes Zeus the guarantor of crops; Hesiod the court adversary becomes Hesiod the poetic adversary; Aphrodite with her stealing and lies is replaced by Demeter with her giving and truth; spring flowers yield to grain; Pandora and the threatened maiden Dike become the protected winter maiden and finally the suitable bride; the Golden Age in which a day's work would last for a year is replaced by the regular pattern of the year's seasons; the bad eating of the δωροφάγοι βασιλεῖς and the rapacious hawk yields to the summer picnic and the ritually proper feast, while the scream on high through the clouds (ὕψι μάλ᾽ ἐν νεφέεσσι 204) of the singer nightingale (ἀηδόνα . . . ἀοιδόν, 203, 208; clearly a pun) becomes the crane's cries on high through the clouds in the fall (ὑψόθεν ἐκ νεφέων 449) and the cicada's summer song (ἀοιδήν 583); the cannibalistic *nomos* of animals is replaced by the farmer's *nomos* itself representing the full cycle of the Almanac (see Bona Quaglia 162). Beyond the general contrast of the two parts there are the formally meaningful contrasts of the centers of the two "heavy parts" with each other: the central digressive Winter section recalls and reverses the story of Pandora and her pithos while the sphragis of the Nautilia recalls and reverses the Heroic Age. Finally, within the second part there are contasts between summer and winter sections and between farming and sailing sections.

Beyond these contrasts, the poem is unified by at least three patterns of regular development: Pandora, time and the individual. All have been discussed in some detail in the last chapter, but the third is worth elaborating here since it is the most comprehensive of them all. We begin with the cosmic separation of good and bad Eris, whose essential difference is whether the individual affects others or only himself. The Prometheus Story has the gods fighting while the Ages Myth brings us down to the creation of the present generation. The set of imperatives that follows focuses on the city and the relation between individuals in city and family, extended over space and time. In the second half we begin with the individual and his immediate surroundings, friends, neighbors, brother. The spatial and temporal frame narrows even further in the Almanac and Nautilia where the presence of others is minimal (hired workers, talkers at the smithy, boat-owner) and the emphasis is on self-sufficiency. The injunctions after the Calendar and the Days mark the end and describe actions that are precisely defined and totally within an individual's control.

These two kinds of contrapuntal order, contrast and linear development, give rise to an extremely complex total structure, one whose richness has only been partially explained here. It is hoped that these findings will encourage others to explore the intricacies of this fascinating poem.

## Appendix 1
## KETO'S BROOD

Three different solutions have been proposed to the problems of the "monster catalogue" in the *Theogony* since West concluded (244) that "the details of the genealogy are not quite certain." These three, taken together, provide a stemma that is more probable and less surprising than West's and suggests as well that the monster catalogue is of fundamental importance to the whole *Theogony*. Surprisingly they have been ignored in the most recent treatment of the poem's form (Thalmann 25).

The problem is to decide to whom the pronoun ἡ δέ refers as (a) the mother of Echidna (295), (b) the mother of Chimera (319) and (c) the mother of Phix and the Nemean lion (326). West's answer to (a) is that she is

> probably Keto, not Medusa (Clericus) or Kallirhoe (Wolf, Preller-Robert), whose only child is Geryoneus in 979ff. Neither Poseidon nor Chrysaor would make an appropriate father for Echidna, and in fact Phorkys is her father in Pherec. 3 F 7. (249)

He is less certain about (b). The arguments he gives for Echidna (254) are first the contrast of ἡ δέ (319) with τὴν μέν in 316 (but "this is not decisive, for the real contrast to τὴν μέν is the new monster Χίμαιραν"), and secondly that "Chimaera's association with Lycia gives her a slight link with Typhon, who was also located in Asia Minor among other places." In favor of the hydra (254f) is first "the careful articulation of Echidna's offspring . . . intended to bind them together as a group, from which Chimaera would be excluded" and secondly that "in this case the mother is the monster last mentioned" as in 326. For (c) West (256) decides that "it is much more likely that Orthos mates with Chimaera" rather than Echidna, who would thereby have "abandoned her husband to lie with her son—unnecessary and unparalleled behaviour" (256). Also this ἡ δέ is analogous to that in 319.

Lemke takes issue especially with West's argument (taken from Abramowicz) about "unparalleled behaviour" which he calls "christlich-ethische" (51). He says that all three pronouns refer to Keto. For the mother of Echidna (a) he accepts West's arguments against Medusa and Kallirhoe and adds that Medusa is in no shape to produce

a second brood and that Keto's name "zur Mutter der Echidna prä-
destiniert" (49). Similarly the possibilities other than Keto for the
mother of Chimera (b) must be eliminated: it cannot be Echidna because her offspring are carefully numbered, nor can it be the hydra
since the ἡ δέ of 319 must be in contrast with the τὴν μέν of 316, who
is the hydra. Also in that case a father would be lacking. Likewise the
mother of Phix and the Nemean lion (c) cannot be Echidna since
having been eliminated as the mother of Chimera she is out of the
picture while Chimera is eliminated by the μὲν / δέ argument used
against the hydra. Therefore only Keto is left once again. Positive
arguments for Keto are (1) the same pronoun ἡ δέ used in all three
cases now refers to the same person; (2) in each case the pronoun
follows the death of "der bisher aufgezählten Nachkommenschaft
von Phorcys und Keto" (52); and (3) the specific mention of Keto's
last child (333) makes it sound as if the discussion has been of her all
along.

Siegmann independently arrived at much the same solution as
Lemke.[1] He thinks that Keto must be the mother of both Echidna (a)
and Chimera (b) and adds that the parents of both must be obvious
or Hesiod is not being clear and the obvious parents are Phorcys and
Keto. Siegmann follows West, however, in thinking that Chimera not
Keto is the mother of Phix and the Nemean lion (c). He argues that
since a new father is named the mother must be the one previously
mentioned, just as above with Typhaon (306). With this arrangement
all three of Keto's offspring after the first set are called snakes (and
are the only ones so called), all three lines are carried to the second
generation, and that second generation is terminated by Heracles
killing the last named.[2]

A year later, Schwabl, who had the benefit of both previous dis-
cussions, disagreed completely.[3] He argues that Echidna's mother (a)
is Kallirhoe because ἡ δέ should refer to what immediately precedes.[4]
He notes that there is a polarity (mortal/immortal) operating in this
line: mortal Medusa versus her immortal sisters; mortal Chrysaor versus immortal Pegasus, and therefore mortal Geryon needs an immortal counterpart, which must be the immortal Echidna. Finally, in the
*Hymn to Apollo* the snake associated with Typhoeus (mate of Echidna
in the *Theogony*) is killed by Apollo (whose epithet is sometimes Χρυσ-
άωρ) next to a καλλίρροος spring (300) and so Kallirhoe is a fitting
mother for snaky Echidna. He argues that the mother of Chimera (b)
is Echidna since the hydra is dead, and so we have the death of the

hydra (τὴν μέν 316) balancing the birth of Chimera (ἡ δέ 319) just as the death of Geryon (τὸν μέν 289) balances the birth of Echidna (ἡ δέ 295). Also, the hydra cannot be the mother of Chimera because of the μὲν / δέ contrast. Thus we have an alternation of monster born (287), monster killed (289), monster born (295), which is expanded: born (313), killed (316), born (319), killed (325), born (326), killed (332). Schwabl argues finally that the mother of Phix and the Nemean lion (c) must be Echidna since their birth is parallel to Chimera's in number of lines and since their deaths are narrated in one line. The oddity of Echidna mating with her son is marked by the unique φασι (306).

Schwabl's argument can be quickly dismissed. His discusion although sometimes extremely suggestive is both subjective and circular: one cannot rest one's conclusions on patterns that only appear if one grants those conclusions. Hesiod has not indicated Kallirhoe's snaky aspect; the actual mention of snakes supports Siegmann's analysis. The strong arguments made by others against the first two of Schwabl's three answers, arguments he does not refute, suggest that his idea of a catalogue's workings is too rigid.

West, Lemke and Siegmann all agree that the mother of Echidna (a) is Keto. Similarly Keto is the likely solution as the mother of Chimera (b). West was dissatisfied with the other alternatives but he did not consider Keto; the additional arguments of both Lemke and Siegmann render the other two very unlikely candidates. The choice for the mother of Phix and the Nemean lion (c) is considerably more difficult. The arguments for Keto are (1) the same pronoun will refer to the same person; (2) ὁπλότατον (333) suggests that we have been thinking of Keto all along; (3) Chimera has been killed and so is an unlikely mother; (4) the μὲν / δέ contrast rules out Chimera. The arguments for Chimera are (1) this is not the time for a mother to mate with her grandson, as Keto would be doing; (2) a new father requires that there either be no new mother (i.e., Chimera) or that the mother be specified (which she is not); (3) with Chimera as mother a clear pattern emerges: three offspring of Keto carried to the second generation have a line ended by Heracles.

When examined, the arguments of Siegmann for Chimera seem stronger than Lemke's for Keto. Against Lemke one can say (1) that these three examples of the pronoun are not the only ones (304 being a fourth), and with Chimera as Phix's mother two will refer to Keto and two to her offspring (ABAB order); (2) Keto has been in mind

whether she or Chimera is the mother; the last child of Gaia, too, is
mentioned after a long gap (821). (3) Medusa after her decapitation
produced offspring and so did Orthos even after his death had been
mentioned. The sticking point is the contrasting particles of 325f, but
it should be noted that repeatedly in the catalogues of the *Theogony* a
break is eased by joining the separate parts with such a combination:
263ff, 336f and 498ff are three clear examples and our three ques-
tionable mothers may be three more. That is to say (with West) that
the contrast may be more generalized than just the subjects of the two
sentences. More important, there is at least one example of this combination with a pronoun that refers to the same subject (83f). Also
only with this argument is there chronological uniformity in the catalogue: Pegasus is associated with Keto's child Medusa and therefore
Chimera, with whom he is associated, should also be Keto's child. Similarly Heracles is involved with the generation following Medusa
(Geryon) and so the hydra should be the generation following Chimera. A chart will clarify this:

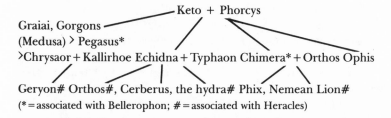

Graiai, Gorgons
(Medusa) > Pegasus*
>Chrysaor + Kallirhoe  Echidna + Typhaon  Chimera* + Orthos  Ophis

Keto + Phorcys

Geryon# Orthos#, Cerberus, the hydra# Phix, Nemean Lion#
(* = associated with Bellerophon; # = associated with Heracles)

    A final argument concerns the implications of Siegmann's anal-
ysis. It is Heracles who brings to an end each attempt by Keto and
Phorcys to produce monsters. The suppression of Heracles' involvement with the other monsters reinforces this impression. In the
larger context of the whole poem, Heracles takes a medial position
between the harmony and peace pictured in the description of Zeus
and the kings of the prologue and Zeus's final battle against the last
claimant to his throne, the monster Typhoeus, who shares his terrible,
fiery and snaky aspect *only* with Heracles' foes.

## Appendix 2
## THE DOUBLE CROWNING

Hesiod's description of the making of the first woman in the *Theogony* seems to contain a doublet since she is crowned first by Athena with crowns of flowers and then by Hephaestus with a crown of gold, ornamented with many figures (576–584). Critics have generally preferred the gold crown, but an equally strong case has been made for the flower crowns and several German critics recently have decided that both passages are interpolated. The dilemma might best be resolved by recognizing that Hesiod meant what the manuscripts have him say, that she was crowned doubly. For this there is a literary argument and an archaeological parallel.

F. A. Wolf (1783) seems to have been the first to question the double crowning and his solution was to excise 576–77. He was followed by Dindorf (1825), Eissner (1823) Kinkel (1870), Lehrs (1870), Flach (1878), Rzach (1913), Mazon (1928), West (1966), Schwabl (1966) and Marg (1970). Wolf's argument was simply that the woman's headgear should be textile, *ut a Minerva donata* and that later the other lines were added since *non satis culta Pandora visa est.* He cautioned, however, that we know little about the woman's world of that time. Robert added that flowers are totally foreign to Athena and that the lines must have been modelled on WD 75.[5]

The crowning with flowers has had its defenders. Goettling (1831) argued that they are appropriate to a bride and he pointed to the second *Hymn to Aphrodite* (VI) vv. 7, 18 for parallels. He added that the two crowns are easily explained by Attic myth *in quo Minerva cum Vulcano coniungitur.* F. A. Paley (1883) noted that WD 74f has the same account and that there Athena is in charge of the entire decoration and concluded that the lines of the second crowning (578ff) are "probably taken from a different recension, in which they stood *in place of* the distich preceding." Friedländer and Schwartz agreed (see Sellschopp 55), while Solmsen (1970) bracketed the second crowning not the first. West more recently in his edition of the *Works and Days* has allowed for the possibility that 576–77 are genuine but "inserted later" (162).

The trend in 20th Century German scholarship has been to regard *both* crownings as interpolated. Sellschopp (55f) objects that flower crowns are unHomeric and first appear in the post-Homeric cycle (i.e., *Kypria* fr.5, *Hymn to Dionysus* [VII] 41) whereas before they are metal (e.g. the second *Hymn to Aphrodite* [VI] 7). Her second objection is that Athena is not associated with flowers in epic. She argues that 581–84 are derived from Homer and that Zeus is clearly the subject of 585 and so should be introduced before. Lendle (34ff) adds that the plurality of the flower crowns shows that the passage is derived from the *Kypria* fragment where there is a plurality of goddesses to bestow the plurality of crowns.[6] He argues against the *Works and Days* passage as a parallel by noting the change from crowns to necklaces and concluding that the writer of WD 72–76 "obgleich er natürlich nicht erkannte, dass der Theogonietext um eine Rhapsodensvariante erweitert war, stutze er doch vor der sachlichen Unmöglichkeit" of the double crowning (38). He agrees with Sellschopp on the inauthenticity of 581–84 also, adding to her arguments that the passage depends on the first *Hymn to Aphrodite* (V) 4f, which is better suited to its context, and that 581 was clearly influenced by and so later than 575.[7]

The basic problem seems to be the double crowning itself. There are good reasons justifying both crowns and it is difficult to decide which is genuine. The flowers suggest marriage, adornment to make the bride sexually attractive. Flowers are repeatedly associated with marriageable women in Greek poetry, whether they are compared to flowers, as in Sappho,[8] or are seduced among flowers like Persephone,[9] or have flowers spring up at their seduction like Hera. The sexual quality of flowers is not absent from the *Theogony*: Poseidon sleeps with Medusa "in a soft meadow among spring flowers" (279). Also Athena's part in the ornamenting is supported by 587.

The gold crown also fits well. It is the natural culmination of the dressing and is a standard element in such scenes.[10] Gold marks the godlike quality of the creature. The marvelous nature of the crown is in keeping with its talented craftsman and the monstrous figures are suggestive of Aphrodite (cf. the first *Hymn to Aphrodite* [V] 4f) and womankind (cf. the first stasimon of *Choephoroi*, Semonides fr. 7 West). Also the control of beasts by means of τέχνη fits with the developing nature of Zeus's order, as argued above, where we also found reason for the joining of Hephaestus and Athena in this regard.[11]

Beyond the literary value of the double crowning, there is an archaeological parallel for it. A well-known calyx krater by the Niobid painter[12] shows on the upper band Pandora facing front in the center of a group of gods. Her stiff wooden pose suggests her lifelessness; her frontality marks her off from the others. Athena, identified by her spear, stands at her right holding a crown of flowers and on Pandora's head is a band of some sort, identified by Smith as a "dotted fillet."[13] In fact it is almost certainly a metal crown. Its design seems too complicated for a simple headband and it is too high for a fillet. Secondly the ties seen at the back of Pandora's head are not the same material as the crown and resemble a style of metal crown that is quite familiar.[14]

Appendix 3
THE EPILOGUE

Virtually no critic considers the end of the *Theogony* genuine:

Aly, Jacoby, and Schwenn take it to 929, Wilamowitz apparently to 939 (*Hesiodos' Erga*, pp. 6,7, n. 1), Goettling, Paley, A. Meyer and J. Schwartz (*Pseudo-Hesiodeia*, p. 435) to 962, Heyne, Sittl, Robert, Bethe (*Die gr. Dichtung* p. 57), and Mazon to 964. I believe that it goes not further than 900. (West 398)

To this list may be added: Schmid 259 (964); Brown 80 n. 44 (955); Solmsen 56 n. 186 (929 or 962); van Groningen 266 (964), Kirk 75 (937), Bradley 44 (964), Marg 21 (955), Nagy 54 (963) and Northrup 8 (955). Walcot (xiii) is evidently unwilling to expunge anything while Schwabl, although repeatedly refusing to speak in these terms, ultimately concludes that we are compelled "an den zugrundeliegenden Plan zu glauben." (137)

We might consider Schwabl's "defense" first. The "basic plan" is that Titanomachy and Tartarus unite to form a 203 line block, as do Typhoeus episode and what follows, and, as the two battles are balanced, so the picture of dark Tartarus is balanced by a picture of bright Olympus:

Die Titanomachie geht danach der Einrichtung der Unterwelt, die Typhonomachie der Entfaltung und Beschreibung der Welt, in der Zeus Götterkönig ist, voraus . . . Überhaupt wird man neben dem Kontrast, den die Welt des Olympos zur Welt des Tartaros bildet, das starke Hervortreten der Kinder von Lichtmächten (Helios, Eos) in den Endabschnitten der Theogonie als Gegensatz zur Schilderung des Nachtbereichs in der Unterweltsbeschreibung auffassen müssen. (137–38)

Schwabl also notes the way Aphrodite is first mentioned with Typhoeus (822) and then recurs in a numerically regular pattern.

The parallelism between Typhoeus and the Titanomachy is indisputable and at first this analysis seems more convincing than some of Schwabl's other claims, but there are problems. First, he must include the transitional ending lines (1019–22) even though they demand the inclusion of the *Catalogue of Women* as well.[15] Second, the relationship between what follows the Titanomachy and what follows the Typhoeus episode is clear only to a degree: the upper world is not "described" as such, rather we have a continuation of genealogical lines. The contrast between dark Tartarus and light Olympus is not emphasized in the text and the prominence of the "Children of Light" depends on doubtful arithmetical schemes. Aphrodite does indeed appear with great frequency in the end (Schwabl cleverly turns an argument against the ending to his advantage), but not in the neat pattern he proposes.[16] We must conclude that Schwabl's scheme, although suggestive, is hardly compelling. The great majority of scholars seem justified in treating 965ff as spurious. The question then becomes whether the poem ends even earlier.

West distills previous scholarship on the question and concludes that "the genuine work of Hesiod . . . goes no further than 900" (398). He gives four reasons:

> (1) Since the *Theogony* leads into the catalogue
> Either Hesiod wrote the *Catalogue* as well as the *Theogony* and wrote them all as one poem; or the end of the *Theogony* as we have it is spurious . . . he cannot have composed the *Catalogue* current in antiquity. And of the lateness of the *Theogony* there are internal indications. (49)
> (2) The end of the *Theogony* contains several mythological statements that it is impossible or gravely implausible to attribute to the age of Hesiod. (398)
> (3) The style becomes
> homogeneously bare and characterless . . . according approximately equal space to each item . . . [it] alludes to events that it refrains from narrating . . . This style sets in suddenly at 901. (398)
> (4) There are no less than four formulae relating to marriage and reproduction which are used two, three, or four times in this section 901–1020, and also in the *Catalogue*, but nowhere else in the *Theogony*. (398)

West's first argument means only that the *Theogony* must end before 1020; it does not tell us where. His second argument finds only one historically doubtful passage in 900–963, the deification of Heracles (950–55):

> He is said to have been first worshipped as a god, as distinct from a hero, at Marathon . . . and the Attic cult seems to have sprung up at about the beginning of the sixth century. (417)

West adds that Heracles never acts like a god but all his deeds are earthly; and that *Iliad* 18.117ff supposes that he died.

None of these points is conclusive. Heracles' new status at Marathon was clearly not a prerequisite for his entry into Olympus. The battle in which he is said to have taken part occurred in 490, but we have a number of 6th Century black-figure vases showing his entry into Olympus.[17] Also, one of the Marathon testimonia states explicitly that when Heracles was burned on Oeta they found no bones and so supposed he had been translated to the gods and therefore made sacrifices to him *as a hero*: ὡς ἥρῳ ποιήσαντες ἁγισμούς (Diodorus 4.39.1). Obviously one does not have to be worshipped as a god when translated to Olympus.

As for Heracles being earth-bound, his deeds may be earthly but his reward is heavenly—eternal youth amid sympotic bliss. The *Iliad* may suppose he dies but the *Odyssey* (11.601ff) has only his εἴδωλον in Hades while he himself is in heaven. This passage is often condemned,[18] but for reasons similar to those being used against the *Theogony* passage. Also, since Heracles in the *Iliad* is a model for Achilles and Achilles is fated to die, there is no place there for Heracles' entry into Olympus.[19] On the other hand, Heracles is not mentioned in the earlier part of the *Theogony* in terms that would make us suspect he will join the gods; the honor his father allows him in releasing Prometheus sounds like an alternative to such translation.

Concerning the stylistic argument, we might note that the homogeneity of the passage reflects the order Zeus has imposed; it could appear only when that order did.[20] Also, allusion instead of full narration can hardly be said to be "un-Hesiodic" in view of 285, 315, 494–96, 502, 513f, 515f, 535, 897f and especially 885.

West's formulaic argument is his strongest, but even here there is room for doubt. Two of the formulae speak of "wife" and we have already seen that Zeus has introduced a social alignment to replace simple generation and by the institution of marriage has neutralized the threat that generation always poses. Thus the word "wife" occurs only twice before the epilogue, and one of those instances (608, of mortals) looks to the future.[21] The other two formulae deal with φιλότης and here West's point seems stronger. In terms of meaning there are other formulae at hand to express the same idea; the question then becomes whether these formulae are comparable in metrical shape as well. They are not: the only possible metrical redundancy is

> μιγήμεναι ἐν φιλότητι (306)
> μιγεῖσ' ἐρατῇ φιλότητι (970, 1009, 1018)[22]

but 306 has a different grammatical function and is crucial to the sentence's syntax whereas the others are simple modifiers.

By 1970 Schwabl had reconsidered his position: he makes two points against the portion after 930.[23] First he argues that earlier the genealogies are always patrilinear but after 938 they often are matrilinear. Since West has argued just the opposite, that the genealogies are basically matrilinear in the beginning, one may doubt Schwabl's assertion. He is forced to explain away a large number of exceptions.[24] It is just as easy, I think, to explain away the exceptions to the matrilinear order. Many of the exceptions are Oceanids: Doris, Electra, Kallirhoe, Styx, Klymene, Metis and Eurynome (but not Eurybia, Eos, Themis, Mnemosyne and Leto). Obviously it was important to keep the Oceanids as a group,[25] and in all but one case the poet has indicated that they are children of Oceanus and so in effect has repeated their genealogy. The one exception is a wife of Zeus, Metis, and we might note that several of Zeus's other wives are also out of place: Themis, Mnemosyne and Leto. Clearly Zeus has overridden the genealogical order to pick his wives. Only two exceptions are left unexplained, Eurybia and Eos. On the other hand, there are three obvious exceptions to a patrilinear order: Typhaon, Orthos and Perses.

Schwabl's second point is much stronger and seems to me the most cogent single reason for doubting what follows 929:

> Theogonie 116–937 kein in genealogischem Zusammenhang genanntes Wesen vorkommt, das nicht eine vollständige genealogische Ableitung erfahren hätte . . . der Stammbaum eines jeden Wessens, sowohl über die väterliche als auch über die mütterliche Linie bis zur Gaia (bzw. zum Chaos) zurückverfolgt werden kann. Ab 938 ist dies nicht mehr der Fall. (444)

A few minor objections might be added: (a) Hermes as messenger of the gods (939) seems odd in view of the use of Iris in the Styx passage (the gods of the *Iliad* use Iris; those of the *Odyssey* use Hermes).[26] (b) The inclusion of Poseidon (930) is justified since he is one of the three major gods[27] but Helios' lineage seems included simply to lead to the birth of Medea and reflects interest in the Argonautica as the later inclusion of Odysseus, Achilles and Aeneas looks to other parts of the cycle.[28] (c) Minos (948) is the son of Zeus in the *Iliad* (14.322); it is odd that this is not mentioned here. (d) The order in 930ff has no easy explanation. (e) Only at 933 is a new lineage not begun at the beginning of a verse (West 415).

## Appendix 4
## REPETITIONS IN THE WORKS AND DAYS

From Krafft's list of repetitions in the Works and Days twenty seven should be excluded as non-distinctive, either because they have too little content or because their core words are repeated frequently (in or outside one or more formulae):

### 1. Minimal Content

#20: ἀλλ' ἔμπης (142, 179*)

#24: αὐτὰρ ἐπεί (83, 121, 140, 156, 728)

#106: αἴ κ' ἐθελ- (209, 268)

#123: μάλα πολλά (696, 697*)

#162 (=963): ἐπὶ χρόνον (133, 326, 754)

#911: νόσφιν ἄτερ (91, 113)

#916: ἄλλοτε δ' ἀλλοῖος (483, 824*)

#1043: ἀλλά νυ καὶ τῶν (513, 684*)

#1046: αὐτὰρ ἐπὴν δή (600, 614)

(* = formula varied beyond shift in case)

### 2. Frequent Occurrence

#30: ἐν θυμῷ (297, 491)

#131: τὸ πρῶτον (291, 679) cf. #129 τ'αγα πρῶτα (387, 467)

#137: νύκτας τε καὶ ἤματα (385, 562)

#160: ἐνὶ θρεσί (107, 531) cf. #165 μετὰ φρεσίν (274, 688) and #531 φρεσὶ ᾗσιν (47, 381)

#246: θεοῖς οἱ Ὄλυμπον ἔχουσιν (139, 257) cf. #265 Ὀλύμπια δώματ' ἔχοντες (81, 110, 128)

#312: ἀπείρονα γαῖαν (160, 487)

#322: θνητῶν τ' ἀνθρώπων (108*, 123, 253) cf. #343 (=731) μερόπων ἀνθρώπων (109, 143, 180)

#364 (=234) ἐπὶ χθονὶ πουλοβοτείρῃ (157, 252, 510)

#413: ἔνδον ἐόντας (452, 476*)

#434: θυμὸν ἔχουσιν (13, 112*, 170*, 340*)

#437: ἱερὸν ἦμαρ (770, 819)

#495: πολλὸν ἀμείνω (19, 320)

#520: ἐπὶ ἔργῳ (444, 549*)

#693: χαλεποῖσι . . . ἐπέεσσι (186*, 332)

#772: τεῷ ἐνικάτθεο (27, 627)

#913: τὸν φθάμενος (554, 570*)

#952: εἰν οἴκῳ (364, 407) cf. #1048 ἔνδοθι οἴκου (523, 601, 733)

#1002 (=962): Διὸς παρὰ μητιόεντος (51, 769), cf. #553 Ζεὺς Κρονίδης (138, 158, 168)

Six repetitions occur in such close proximity that they are probably simply verbal reflexes:

#220: διάκτορος Ἀργειφόντης (68, 77)

#665: μεθ' ὁμήλικας (444, 447)

#828: σθένος Ὠρίωνος (598, 615, 619*)

#920: ἐσθλὴ δ' ἀνδρογόνος (788, 794)

#955: πλείοτη δὲ χάρις (720, 723*)

#1052: οὐ διάῃσιν (517, 519)

Of the remaining forty-five, forty-three have been or can be explained by the present study as emphasizing either the structure of the poem or its themes (especially the Pandora themes of stupid brother and dangerous woman):

#139: πόλεμόν τε κακὸν καί (14, 161*)

πόλεμον occurs only twice and once in another form. Here the Ages Myth, specifically the Golden Age, is being joined to bad Eris. See above p. 56.

#318 (=186=281): ζείδωρος ἄρουρα (117, 173, 237)

ἄρουρα occurs 6 times, ζείδωρος occurs only 3 times, joining the ideal world before Pandora (117), in the Golden Age (173) and in the just city (237). See above p. 53. The other occurrences of ἄρουρα (428, 461, 463) describe the practical ideal of the present.

#346: οἰκόνδε νέεσθαι (554, 673)

νέεσθαι in any form occurs only twice, οἰκόνδε only twice; in both places, one is encouraged to return home quickly since the weather is bad. The repetition joins Almanac and Nautilia.

#419: εὐρέα πόντον (507, 650)

πόντον in some form occurs 12 times, which may seem to preclude significant repetition but 9 of the repetitions are in the Nautilia and the others seem to be in significant relation to that section: 247, the Trojan War (see above p. 68); 507, the winter digression (see above p. 72); 817, the end of the Days. 247, 507 and 650 (the sphragis of the Nautilia) are further connected by having the only occurrences of εὐρύς in any form.

#515: ὥς σε κελεύω (316, 536, 623)

κελεύω occurs in any form only 3 times; its structural function has been described above p. 00.

#569 (=921): ἠέρα ἐσσάμενοι (125, 223, 255)

ἐσσάμενοι in all forms occurs 4 times (plus περιέσσασθαι 530), ἠέρα 3 times. The significant repetitions are discussed at #1073. I can think of no reason to connect the need to cloak oneself (536, 539) against the winter wind (549) with the guardians, cloaked in mist (125, 255).

#593: βουσὶ καὶ ἡμιόνοισιν (607, 816)

βουσί occurs in all forms 23 times but ἡμιόνοισιν only 3 times, binding together introduction (46), end of Almanac (607) and end of Days (816).

#710: λιγυρὴν . . . ἀοιδήν (583, 659)

This formula joins the summer hiatus and sailing digression. At the same time it is part of a larger pattern which moves from the Muses' song of Zeus (1), through the competing bards (26), the endangered singer-nightingale (208), to the victorious Hesiod (659, 662). See p. 86. This plus 583 (see p. 65) are all the occurrences of the ἀοιδ/ἀειδ- stem.

#789: ἀεσίφρονα θυμόν (315, 335, 646)

θυμόν in some form occurs 21 times in the poem; the distinctive epithet ἀεσίφρονα occurs only 3 times in any form, always in an address to Perses. See above p. 74 and below #915.

#812: καὶ σχέτλια ἔργα (124, 238, 254)

ἔργα in all forms occurs 35 times; σχέτλια occurs only 5 times, connecting bad Eris (15), with the Iron Age (187) and the unjust city (238) on the one hand, and the watchers against injustice on the other (124, 254; see below #1073).

#822: μινύθουσι δὲ οἶκοι (244, 325*) cf. ἀρίζηλον μινύθει 6

οἶκος occurs in some form 20 times; forms of μινύθουσι occur only 5 times, connecting Zeus's punishment in the proem (6, echoed in 325, see above p. 61) and against the unjust city (244).

#830: τροπὰς ἠελίοιο (479*, 564, 663)

τροπάς occurs 3 times in all forms, marking the two parts of the Almanac and Nautilia. See p. 71.

#846: ἐγγύθι ναίει (288, 343, 700)

ἐγγύθι occurs 4 times, ναίει in all forms 8 times. The meaningful formula seems to be #1070 (see below). A related form, ἐγγύθι ναιετάουσ' 389, seems to carry no special meaning.

#848: ἔργα νέμονται (119*, 231)

For ἔργα see above #812. νέμονται in all forms occurs 3 times, joining Golden Age (119) and just city (231, contrasted with unjust city, οὐχ ἰθεῖαν ἔνειμαν 224). See above p. 63.

#868: πάντα νοήσας (267, 293)*

πάντα occurs 12 times, νοήσας in all forms 8 times. See p. 83 for the thematic complex of which this is a part, and see below on #985.

#884: μέγ' ὄνειαρ (41, 346, 822)

ὄνειαρ occurs only 3 times. The end of the poem is meant to recall and revise the beginning of the first part (see p. 83).

#889: κεχρημένον ἄνδρα κομίζει (317, 500)

The key word κεχρημένον occurs 4 times in all forms. For the formula see p. 58.

#914: ὧδ' ἔρδειν(35, 382, 760)

ἔρδειν occurs 6 times in all forms of the ἐρδ- stem (3 more from the ἐργ- stem). Structurally the formula marks the introduction (35), the beginning of the Calendar proper (382) and the end of the second part, just before the Days (760).

#915: ὦ Πέρση (27, 213, 274, 611, 641*)

ὦ by itself is found nowhere else; Πέρση in all forms is found 10 times. The name marks structural units. See p. 74 and see on #1032.

#917: ἀρχομένον δὲ πίθου (368, 815*)

πίθου occurs 6 times in all forms, all of which have to do with "opening" and all of which are part of the Pandora theme. See p. 84.

#926: πρωτογόνων δ' ἐρίφων (543, 592*)
ἐρίφων occurs 3 times in all forms, the third occurrence (786) joining the Days to the Almanac.

#928: αἵδε γὰρ ἡμέραι εἰσί (769, 822*)
This formula clearly rings the Days (see p. 81), although no word is distinctive (ἡμέρη occurs 4 times in all forms; ἦμαρ 20 times).

#938: καὶ κύνα καρχαρόδοντα (604, 796)
κύνα in all forms occurs only twice; for its function see p. 84.

#947: ψεύδεά θ'αἱμυλίους τε λόγους (78, 789)
ψεύδεα and αἱμυλ- in all forms occur only twice. For their use, see p. 75. The verb ψεύδομαι occurs twice (283, 709), both times connected with brothers (274, 707) and so part of the Pandora theme.

#960: καὶ οἰζύος (113, 177)
οἰζύος in all forms occurs only twice, connecting the evils of Pandora (113) with those of the Iron Age (177), the inverse of #318. The adjective οἰζυρός (195, 639) joins Ascra to these examples of bad Eris. See p. 68.

#967: (= 442): ἀνθρώποισιν ἐμήσατο κήδεα λυγρά (49, 95*)
κήδεα occurs twice in all forms, λυγρά 6 times. Pandora carries out Zeus's plan. See p. 49.

#983: Δημήτερος ἱερὸν ἀκτήν (466, 597, 805)
ἀκτήν in all forms is found only 4 times, the fourth being the similar phrase Δημήτερος ἀκτήν 32. Good Eris (32) is realized in the two parts of the Almanac (466, 597) and then in the Days (805).

#985: (= 147, 345): Ζηνὸς νόος αἰγιόχοιο (483, 661) cf. #159 Διὸς νόον (105)
Forms of Ζεύς occur 24 times; νόος in all forms occurs 10 times, all of which seem to be related: 67 refers to Pandora; 373 to the Pandora-like woman; 105, 483, 661 to Zeus's νόος, ineluctable in 105, hard to know in 483, known by the poet in 661 (see above p. 83). Man's νόος, independent of Zeus, is described first in its folly (260, 323, 685), then in an injunction to good νόος (714) and finally with the birth of a man of good νόος (793). See p. 83.

#988: θέρεος καματώδεος ὥρη (584, 664*)
θέρεος in all forms occurs 6 times, καματώδεος twice (plus κάματος 177, 305) and ὥρη 7 times. For the formula see on p. 66.

#996: τεκμαίρεται εὐρύοπα Ζεύς (229, 239)

For Ζεύς see above on #985. τεκμαίρεται occurs twice in all forms, plus διετεκμήραντο 398. The formula contrasts the just and the unjust cities.

#999: ἀκηδέα θυμὸν ἔχοντες (112, 170)

For θυμόν see #789; ἀκηδέα occurs only twice. The formula is akin to #318, the inverse of #960 (cf. also #967).

#1017: ὑπὲρ καπνοῦ καταθεῖο (45, 629*)

The formula is more properly, πηδάλιον . . . ὑπὲρ καπνοῦ. καπνοῦ occurs twice. For the formula see p. 51.

#1022 (= 382): βίος ἄρκιος εἴη (501, 577)

βίος occurs 9 times in all forms, ἄρκιος 4 times. The formula juxtaposes lazy chatter (501) with hard work (577). See p. 70.

#1028: καὶ δῆριν ὀφέλλει (14, 33*)

δῆριν occurs twice in all forms, connecting Hesiod's court case to bad Eris (see p. 60).

#1029: καὶ ἐπίκλοπον ἦθος (67, 78)

ἦθος occurs 3 times in all forms, ἐπίκλοπον twice, connecting Zeus's command and its execution.

#1032: μέγα νήπιε Πέρση (286, 633) cf. #60 νήπιος οὐδὲ τὸ οἶδ' (456) and #87 νήπιοι οὐδὲ ἴσασιν (40)

See on #915. For this aspect of the Pandora theme see p. 83.

#1033: μεμνημένος εἶναι/ ὡραίου (616f, 641f)

Since both μεμνημένος and ὡραι- stems occur 7 times, this may not fit any pattern, but see n. 2 p. 118 for the theme of memory.

#1036: πιμπλῇσι καλιήν (301, 307*, 411)

πιμπλῇσι in all forms occurs twice (plus πλήθωσι 307), καλιήν 5 times, all of which are significant (see p. 70).

#1037: σκολιῇσι δίκῃσιν (219, 250)

σκολιῇσι occurs 8 times in all forms, δίκῃσιν 24 times. In addition to this formula, the words occur together in 221, 262, 264 but seem to serve little purpose beyond characterizing the world of bad Eris.

#1044: ἀλλὰ σ' ἄνωγα/ φράζεσθαι (403f, 687f).

ἄνωγα occurs in all forms 4 times: this formula, a similar formula (#213 σε φράζεσθαι ἄνωγα 367) and v. 68 describing Epimetheus. For the paralleling of Perseus and Epimetheus via this formula see p. 83. φράζεσθαι occurs 8 times in all forms.

#1055 (= #329): αὐτὰρ ἐπεὶ καὶ τοῦτο γένος κατὰ γαῖα κάλυψεν (121*, 140, 156)

This full-line formula marks the parallelism of the first three Ages (see p. 50).

#1070: τὸν δὲ μάλιστα καλεῖν, ὅστις σέθεν ἐγγύθι ναίει (343, 700*)

For the importance of this full-line formula see p. 75.

#1073: φύλακες θνητῶν ἀνθρώπων/ οἵ ῥα φυλάσσουσίν τε δίκας καὶ σχέτλια ἔργα/ ηέρα ἑσσάμενοι, πάντη φοιτῶντες ἐπ' αἶαν (123–5, 253–5).

See above on #569 and #812. For defense of this two line formula see p. 62.

One formula remains which has no obvious structural function:

#241: εὐτροχάλῳ ἐν ἀλωῇ (599, 806)

ἀλωῇ occurs only twice in any form. It may join Days (806) to Almanac (599).

One argues *against* the present analysis:

#944 (= 558): τῷ δὲ θεοὶ νεμεσῶσι (303, 741)

νεμεσῶσι occurs only 3 times in all forms. It suggests that the first set of injunctions should be extended back before 336 if it is to parallel the second set.

# NOTES TO CHAPTER TWO

[1] Kirk 63. Works referred to more than once are generally cited by the author's last name; the full reference is given in the "Works Repeatedly Cited." Well-known editions are cited simply by author's name. Hesiodic texts are cited from M. L. West's edition of *Theogony* (Oxford 1966) and *Works and Days* (Oxford 1978).

[2] I do not mean to imply that there were *no* unitarians in 1960, just that they did not speak out at the Fondation Hardt.

[3] Walcot presented an earlier version of his analysis in *CQ* 6 (1956) 205f. I pass over Schwabl's arithmetical scheme, which has been sufficiently criticized by reviewers. See especially West *CR* 18 (1968) 27; Vos *Mnemosyne* 22 (1969) 430; Combellack *CP* 64 (1969) 121. For examples of his method see appendices 1 and 3.

[4] His analysis has been accepted by Said 209f.

[5] Bradley 44 offers much the same scheme, which he finds already outlined in the proem: first gods 116–382; Zeus' allies 383–452; god and man 453–616; Zeus' enemies 617–885; last gods 886–964. This is hardly more precise than speaking of beginning, middle and end.

[6] Brown omitted the Typhoeus episode because he was following the *communis opinio* at the time *not* because he was trying to make his pattern neater.

[7] In this last principle, West was anticipated by Schmid 261f. See also C. Robert, "Zu Hesiods Theogonie," *Melanges Nicole* (Geneva 1905) 478 (= Heitsch 166). I leave out of the discussion West's principle #5, the last god is sometimes called "youngest," and #6, describing the various combinations of parents in 940ff.

[8] But West does use length as a criterion elsewhere, arguing (244) that the Echidna passage is out of place because of its length. Yet ring structure guarantees it:
(a) Phorcys and Keto 270
(b) Hesperides 275
(c) Pegasus 281
(d) Geryon and Orthos 287–93
(e) Echidna 297
(e) Echidna 304
(d) Orthos and Geryon 309
(c) Pegasus 325
(b) apples (of the Hesperides) 335
(a) Phorcys and Keto 336.
Note that the beginning of the repetition is formally marked by the repetition of her name, often considered awkward (see West *ad* 301). The repetition is part of a fuller ring, as Julia Gaisser points out to me:
θνητοῖς ἀνθρώποις οὐδ' ἀθανάτοισι θεοῖσι, 296
σπῇ ἔνι γλαφυρῷ, 297
description of Echidna, 298–300
ἔνθα δέ οἱ σπέος ἐστί, 301
ταλοῦ ἀπ' ἀθανάτων τε θεῶν θνητῶν τ' ἀνθρώπων, 302.

# NOTES TO CHAPTER THREE

[1] Friedländer was the first to discuss the implications of this; See now Minton, Janko.
[2] Schwabl 24, Janko 21.

[3] West 169 notes that περί with accusative in epic elsewhere has a local meaning and argued for that interpretation here. He has been followed by Bradley (1969) 20 n.31 and Minton 369 n. 23, but not Verdenius (1972) 241, who retains the traditional interpretation "concerning." It makes little difference for the present argument.

[4] Minton (367f) is hardly justified in arguing that the investiture is simply another narrative segment like the "consequent activities" section of a hymn. See also Maehler 37 n. 2 who offers Hymns 6.3ff, 15.4, 20.2 as parallels (of which only the last is at all close), but eventually admits "er das traditionelle Schema vom Inhaltlichen her durchbricht" (38).

[5] Nagy 53f, Griffith 47.

[6] For the formal pecularity of the *Hymn to Apollo* see Minton 376f, Janko 17.

[7] Schwabl (1966) 9, Minton 357, Marquandt 3, Thalmann 135. See also Arthur 107.

[8] Scholars since antiquity have tried to explain what Hesiod means in v.35 (see West), and there is considerable doubt among critics as to what is being dismissed. Given the immediately preceding talk about breathing divine speech into the poet so that he can sing of the future and past, we may plausibly follow the ancient interpretation of the oak as Dodona and the rock as Delphi. At the same time, we should not rule out the wilderness interpretation of Marquandt 4f, Thalmann 142f and others. See further Chapter 3 note 64.

[9] Archilochus Testimonium 4 Tarditi; Callimachus *Aetia* I fr.2 Pf.

[10] For guides to the burgeoning bibliography on the proem see Arthur and Thalmann.

[11] Many have noted this, e.g. Solmsen 65, Siegmann 10.

[12] "Lines 36–39 repeat in inverse order the ideas, and in three instances the phrasing, of lines 31–34" (Thalmann 136, following Schwabl).

[13] Ziegler 1473f shows in detail how 11ff is inappropriate to the *Theogony* (see also von Fritz 34). For a contrasting analysis see especially Schwabl 24, who demonstrates effectively how 11ff is formally bound to the rest.

[14] This is a relatively rare epithet for Hera in epic (2x) but a common one for Helen (12x). It never elsewhere occurs in a different line than the proper name.

[15] δεύτερον 47 means that Zeus is the second theme, not that he takes second place or is narrated only second (see Siegmann 11 and Nagy 55 versus West 172). His power is hymned in both prologue and epilogue, like the Muses, and so 48 (properly emended) may stay. Von Fritz (35f), following Friedländer, says that "second" means hymnic poetry as opposed to heroic epic, but this seems unlikely.

[16] "Occuper l'Olympe et posséder le pouvoir divin sont synonymes" van Groningen 264.

[17] For this equation see Siegmann 11f, Thalmann 139.

[18] For the difficulty with ταῦτ' in 75 see Friedländer 9 n. 14, Aly 27.

[19] I follow Solmsen (OCT 1970, 1983) in keeping 111 and omitting 108–10. For a defense of 111, bracketed by West, see Friedländer 13 n.19 and Mazon (1928) 9 n.2. The pairing of group with single elemental deity in 108–10 (θεοί / γαῖα 108 = earth, ποταμοί / πόντος 109 = water, ἄστρα / οὐρανός 110 = air) seems somewhat artificial and does not fit our *Theogony*: although many of the θεοί are descended from Gaia, the ποταμοί are not descended from Pontos but from Oceanus (337ff), and the only connection between the ἄστρα and Ouranos is his epithet ἀστερόεντα 127. Neitzel (118ff) tries to explain away the discrepancies and defends 108–10 by arguing that the program gives first the second generation (105–7), then the first (108–10) and then the third (111–13), but this requires that τῶν of 111 refer back to 106, which is difficult. For our purposes it makes little difference whether 108–10 are omitted or not since at most they parenthetically describe 116–32a.

[20] Two of Night's children, Day and Aither, are given in 124, probably because Hesiod thought these were early beings who belonged back with the first generations. One could make a structural argument as well, that the interweaving of Night's progeny, like that of Ouranos, binds the genealogical portion of the poem together. Solmsen (1982) 6 explains their early position by their "meteorological" function; West 38 by their lack of progeny. Schwenn says that the split of Night's progeny into two groups separates her sexually produced children from her asexually produced ones (3). It may seem odd that the sexually produced children are listed

first but the latter seem more appropriate after the castration of Ouranos, who used to "bring on the night" (176) before assaulting Gaia.

[21] Schwabl (1970) 441. See also Thalmann 40.

[22] Van Groningen 282; West 426.

[23] See also M. L. West, *The Hesiodic Catalogue of Women* (Oxford 1985) 127.

[24] It is worth noting that these three occur in the same order: Demeter-Harmonia-Medea = birth of Demeter's child-marriage of Harmonia-marriage of Medea.

[25] See also Schmid 261, Mazon 16, Schwenn 49, Kirk 75, and Marg 284.

[26] For the most part. See e.g. Solmsen 39 n. 124, West 405. Solmsen (32) notes that the children represent the "essential qualities of Zeus as ruler."

[27] Vernant (72) therefore overstates his case in saying "le nouveau souverain n'a pas le pouvoir d'immobiliser le temps, d'arrêter le cours des naissances."

[28] We end with an irrelevant genealogy of Helios' children and his grandchild Medea. The only elements that interrupt the story of Dionysus and Heracles are the birth of Hermes by Zeus (938f) and Triton by Poseidon (931–33a). West (414) argues that this last is interpolated: "Hesiod would surely have put such a figure as Triton . . . among the descendants of Pontos."

[29] So words for "wife" (ἄκοιτις, ἄλοχος, παρακοίτη) for the most part occur after the Titanomachy: 410, 608, 886, 921, 928, 937, 946, 948, 953. 608 is referring to the wife of a man not a god.

[30] E.g. Brown 23, Vernant 31. See also Solmsen 55, West 397, Marg 285.

[31] In later tradition is the Thetis who is to be the mother of the dangerous child. Zeus's potential child, by Thetis, is Prometheus' secret in the *Prometheus Bound*; while in Pindar's *Isthmian* 8, Poseidon and Zeus are both dissuaded from producing a child by Thetis, one destined to be stronger than its father. For Thetis's power see L. M. Slatkin, "The Wrath of Thetis," *TAPA* 116 (1986) 1–24.

[32] Contra Vernant (1977) 65. A. Lesky is wrong to say that Hesiod has no interest in Homer's "scenes of married strife in Olympus," *A History of Greek Literature* (London 1966) 6. West notes (402) that the "quarrel between Zeus and Hera is also implicit in *Th.* 924–9, but the logical order of events has been destroyed: Zeus swallows Metis six wives before his marriage with Hera." One should note, however, that this structural device of bracketing Zeus's other mates with the dangerous Metis and Hera at either end gives the danger from Hera an air of permanence. Schoemann 247f argued that this made Zeus a better husband to Hera than Homer's Zeus.

[33] The connection was worked out in detail by H. Usener, "Eine Hesiodische Dichtung," *RhM* 56 (1901) 174–86. See also G. S. Kirk, J. E. Raven and M. Schofield, *The Presocratic Philosophers* (Cambridge 1983²) fr.52.

[34] See now Mondi.

# NOTES TO CHAPTER FOUR

[1] Verdenius (1972) 259; see already Schoemann 246f, who considers the division at Mekone part of the same distribution. See also Ziegler 1490, Mazon (1928) 10, Solmsen 15 n. 31, Kirk 87, and more recently M. Rudhardt *Le Sacrifice dans l'Antiquité* Entretiens Hardt (Geneva 1981) 28, citing Vernant, and R. Mondi, "Tradition and Innovation in the Hesiodic Titanomachy," *TAPA* 116 (1986) 38.

[2] Hesiod seems to use λαγχάνω of the Ouranid generation (203,422,424) and διαδατέομαι (544, 606, 885), δατέομαι (112), and διαιρέω (112) of later times (but see δασμός 425 vs.424). This may suggest a development from primitive allotment to deliberate division (contrast *Iliad* 15.189f).

[3] The change from Ouranos to Zeus is marked by the change in meaning of μήδεα from genital (180, 188, 200) to mental (398, 545, 550, 559, 561).

[4] The term is used of Zeus also at 36,40,53,71,580,896; it is used of Ouranos at 164,165,171,180,207,472?,502?,617? The term is elsewhere used only three times, of Nereus (262), Poseidon (932) and Kronos (73).

[5] See also D. Boedeker "Hecate: A Transfunctional Goddess in the *Theogony?*" *TAPA* 113 (1983) 81.

[6] The parallelism has been often noted, e.g. Aly 35; Pfister 9; Friedländer 13 n. 20; P. Walcot, "Hesiod's Hymns to the Muses, Aphrodite, Styx and Hecate," *SO* 34 (1958) 11f; Griffith 52.

[7] Lendle 119f gives lists of etymologies and word plays.

[8] This was proposed as a serious etymology by Fick (see Heckenbach *RE* s.v. Hekate col. 2769) and W. Prellwitz "Participia praesentis activi in der Zusammensetzung," *Glotta* 17 (1929) 145–47. Schwabl 55 n.7 calls it the ancient etymology. The usual interpretation, however, is that her name is to be related to the epithet of Apollo, ἑκατηβόλος; see now Kraus 14f, G. Derossi, "L'Inno Ecati di Bacchilide (fr 1 B Sn.) e la 'Figura' Arcaica della Dea," *QTLCQ* 2 (1971–74) 16–26, Marg 198, Neitzel 109f. I am gratified to see this interpretation argued by J. S. Clay, "The Hecate of the *Theogony*," *GRBS* 25 (1984) 27–38.

[9] The positive form is found in the variant reading of 730, Διὸς μεγάλοιο ἕκητι.

[10] "Aus der hesiodischen Hekatepartie kann man keine 'Allgottheit' konstruieren; Hekate war dies in Griechenland nie" Kraus 62. See already Pfister 8. One should not overlook the connection of Zeus's mother Rhea ('Ρείη 453) with the immediately preceding occurrences of ῥεῖα (438,443), all at the beginning of the line. Philippson (27) comments on the way the Styx and Hecate are positioned next to each other: "an der Grösse und Machtfülle der also Belehnten erweist sich die Grösse und Machtfülle des Belehnenden." Marg 200f notes "die an allen Göttern teilhabende Gewalt der Hekate, die Durchkreuzung ihrer Bereiche fügt sich wohl zu dem Ausbau des Zeusglaubens, den wir bei Hesiod treffen."

[11] Thus the common complaint against the Typhoeus episode that "Tartarus is not a god in Hesiod" (Solmsen 53 n. 172) has no force. One should note the echo of Tartarus' former self in δειρήν 727.

[12] Solmsen 61; see also Walcot (1966) 46, Schwabl 146, Thalmann 39.

[13] The parallel order is not exact—Hades is mentioned after Styx in the body of the poem (455) and so should come after Styx in Tartarus, but this may be another displacement of the crucial apportionment of the world.

[14] To West's list of critics (383) add Mazon (1928) 15f, Brown 12, Solmsen (1982) 12 (all *con*), Schwabl 106ff, Marg 276 (both *pro*).

[15] So Mazon (1928) 15, Schwenn 42, Solmsen 53 n.172, Kirk 75, West 381. Barron 95f does not think it is out of place.

[16] In fact these winds are contrasted (μὲν . . . δέ) with the natural winds whose genesis is explicitly described as ἐκ θεόφιν (871). West (381, followed by Said 207) argues that the Near Eastern parallel, the tale of Ullikummi, justifies the Typhoeus episode, but Walcot (1966) 9f has questioned this. In any case, Hesiod has not included Typhoeus in the program and so he remains extraneous. Schwabl (1970) 444 looks to Typhaon's mating with Echidna (306) for a genealogy and argues that this guarantees the authenticity of both Typhoeus episode and monster catalogue: "ergibt sich allein aus den genealogischen Verhältnissen auch die Notwendigkeit der Typhonomachie für das ganze Gedicht."

[17] Walcot (1966) 58, West 38, Philips 297.

[18] Solmsen 50. See also Schmid 261, Kirk 88, Vernant (1977) 66. Robert 478 notes that we expect the Titanomachy at 506 while Schwenn 130 argues that this chronological displacement allows the Titanomachy to be the climax and Mondi 333 says it preserves "the genealogical skeleton."

[19] Rearing is distinct from bearing at 192,198,480,582,1001 but perhaps not at 107.

Friedländer *GGA* 193 (1931) 257 (= Heitsch 120) argues that ἐθρέφθη 192 is the same as ἐγένετο. This may be so but the presence of an agent who is not the mother makes such an interpretation impossible for 328.

[20] I have excluded examples which pair god and man (e.g. Zeus, "father of gods and men"), some of which occur in the succession narratives (197, 204, 468, 643).

[21] For example Bradley 45 connects Prometheus with both Ouranos and Kronos while Schwabl (1970) 456 connects him with Ouranos and Vernant (1977) 65ff contrasts Prometheus's struggle against Zeus with the Olympians' struggle against the Titans.

[22] Likewise Vernant 40f, following Apollodorus, and Nietzel 150, "die Gewalt des Zeus *ist* seine in den τέχναι sich zugende Überlegenheit."

[23] See now Mondi 340f. Hesiod may have been trying to minimize the discreditable aspects of the overthrow of Kronos, i.e., the loss of the Golden Age (cf WD 111) and to sidestep the moral question of Zeus's victory over his own father, as Walcot (1966) 60 suggests. Kronos is mentioned in the Titanomachy (which is surely the conflict implied by 73) only as the father of the victorious Olympians. See Vernant 73 for a thorough condemnation of Hesiod's Kronos.

[24] For the subtle relationship between the first woman and bellies see now Arthur.

[25] Walcot (1966) 5 seems to have been the first to observe this.

[26] Sellschopp 74, Verdenius (1972) 244, following West.

[27] The comparison is highlighted by the virtual identity of the line preceding either statement (681 = 849).

[28] Said (208) argues that ὀξὺ νόησε (838) shows the results of Zeus' ingestion of Metis and explains why he no longer needs Gaia's help. See also Vernant 60 n.1.

[29] The connection is even closer since in the *Hymn to Apollo* Hera produces Typhoeus to replace Hephaestus, and Hephaestus is rescued by Thetis (319), who in some stories is to produce a son who would overthrow Zeus. See Chapter 2 n.31.

[30] Verdenius (1971) 5 argues that ἀμφιγυήεις means "handy" and has nothing to do with cripples, but this is not how it was understood in antiquity. One should note also the language of Zeus's threatened expulsion of Hera and Athena in *Iliad* 8.402ff, γυιώσω . . . βαλέω . . . δεκάτους . . . ἐνιαυτούς. Not only do we have the Hesphaestean crippling but the ten years matches the expulsion until the tenth year for gods who perjure themselves (803).

[31] Zeus's superiority to fate is suggested by the immediately following birth of the Fates by Themis (904–6). This should not be viewed as a contradiction of their earlier birth (217) but rather a statement that Zeus is above fate. So Solmsen sees their birth as "a victory over Night . . . a landmark on the road to another and final triumph of Zeus" (38).

[32] χόανος might make one think of the use of that instrument to create matter in Empedocles fr.96. W. K. C. Guthrie, *A History of Greek Philosophy* vol.2 (Cambridge 1965), notes (212 n.1) that in both passages the instrument is a "melting pot" not a "funnel."

[33] The oddness of Tartarus suddenly becoming a father is noted by many, e.g. Schwenn 44, Solmsen 53 n. 172, West 383. Although γαῖα is still monstrous (πελώρη 861), she is contrasted with the clay crucible, "divine earth" (χθονὶ δίη 866), controlled by Hephaestus.

[34] Thus Zeus's ability to win over the Hundred-handers is all the more remarkable, especially since he will send them down to Tartarus (but as the guards not the guarded).

[35] Euripides fr.312 N² says simply that Pegasus pulled Zeus's chariot, which had lightning bolts in it.

[36] On the acceptability of equating Typhaon with Typhoeus see now Said 206f. It may be objected that the mating should precede Typhoeus's immolation, but there is no more natural place for them to meet than Tartarus, and that would follow the immolation. Echidna's cave, after all, is under the earth (304).

[37] At least in the plural (i.e., all but 661, 896), as Professor Henry Johnstone has pointed out to me.

[38] This supports West's reading θυμῷ for βουλῇ in 661. The gods' decree in 960 if genuine is presumably the same. I do not include the local use of βουλή as "council" of the gods in

802. It is not clear how R. Mondi (above n.1) 37 can say that the reference to Zeus's βουλαί in 653 "is sufficiently vague to leave open the possibility that someone else put the idea into his mind in the first place."

[39] For the Lernean hydra's antisocial behavior see Euripides' *Heracles* 420.

[40] See above chapter 1 n.8.

[41] For the problem of who is the mother in 295, 319 and 326 see Appendix 1.

[42] The connection is explicit in [Aeschylus'] *Prometheus* 7, where Hephaestus is reminded that Prometheus stole *his* craft.

[43] Vernant 32 notes Prometheus' essential similarity to Metis (559–887).

[44] Reading τέχνῃσι in 929 with the mss. and West vs. Solmsen (OCT).

[45] For defense of both crownings see Appendix 2.

[46] The monsters on the crown label Woman as monster (see *Choephoroi* 585ff), more universal than the particular and isolated monsters Heracles faces and so truly intermediate between the Typhoeus and Keto episodes.

[47] βασιλεύς is used only of Kronos (476,486) and Zeus (886,897, 923) and, in the plural, of his earthly representatives the kings (80, 82, 88, 96) until the very end (Aeetes 957, 992, Memnon 985, Pelias 995). Similarly the verb is used only of Zeus (883) and the adjective only of Zeus and Kronos (462, 892). ἄναξ, on the other hand, is used not only of Zeus and Kronos but also Prometheus (543), Typhoeus (859), Poseidon (932) and the considerably less threatening Apollo (347) and, in the doubtful portion, Emathion (985). The verb ἀνάσσω, however, is confined to Zeus (403, 491, 506, 883) or potential threats (Typhoeus 837; Hades 850), except in the doubtful portion (1016).

[48] This is further supported by the close juxtaposition of Zeus's apportioning of μοῖρα to Atlas (520) and Prometheus' apportioning of the shares (μοίρας) of the ox (544). See Vernant (1977) 65f.

[49] The Promethean punishments of eagle and column may reflect the Stygean judgment facing divine purjurers: Zeus's messenger (here Iris not the eagle) is sent to Styx, who is surrounded by "silver columns" (779), to fetch water which causes the perjurer to lie speechless for a "great year" (799).

[50] See Robert 477.

[51] Or they are being "distinguished," depending on how one translates ἐκρίνοντο 535; see West 317 and Verdenius (1971) 3.

[52] See Philips 298, Walcot (1966) 81.

[53] Philips 292 analyses Mekone in this way on the basis of Near Eastern parallels. Note that Prometheus is the father of Deukalion in the *Catalogue* (fr.2,3 M-W).

[54] Some critics prefer that οἱ in 301 refer to Echidna's mother (see West 250), but this is difficult.

[55] Tartarus is generally pictured both below the earth and at the ends of the earth (e.g. *Iliad* 8.478), as are Styx (see Schwenn 28) and Atlas, who in the *Theogony* is located both below the earth (746) and at the ends of the earth (518).

[56] The scholiast to *Prometheus* 94 mentions 30,000 years of bondage.

[57] For this problem see Mazon (1928) 54 n. 1, Schwenn 131, Solmsen 47 n. 152. West (313), following Sittl, argues that it is only the killing of the eagle being described in 526ff and so there is no contradiction with 616, which describes the bondage, but this ignores 533 where Zeus stops the anger "which he had before," which clearly contradicts 615f which says Prometheus did not escape Zeus's anger but is chained.

[58] See, most recently, Marquandt 7f, Thalmann 142.

[59] Likewise Hera is now Argive Hera (12). A further possible implicit development may be from the absence of human wit in the Keto narrative, where the destruction of the Sphinx by Oedipus' intelligence is *not* narrated, to the presence of human intelligence here.

[60] "The poet does not play a passive role" Verdenius (1972) 238. Hesiod's part is even greater if we read δρέψασθαι in 31; see Kambylis 65.

[61] See Maehler 39, Kambylis 62f. For a sociological interpretation see Nagy 48f and, at length, Svenbro chapter 1.

[62] Tarditi Testimonium #4 E₁1 col.II vv.27–31. The Epimenides parallel was noted already by Otto, according to Kambylis 62.

[63] There may be a pun on λόχος suggesting "womb" as well as "ambush." The unusual λοχέοιο in 178 supports this possibility. M. L. Lang points me to κευθμῶνι (158) as well.

[64] Plato's *Phaedrus* 275 b8 seems a convincing parallel. The scholia offered this as one explanation (see West 168) as did Goettling in his 1843 edition. Recently Bradley (1969) 22, with this interpretation as his basis, has generalized the reference to mean "the traditional gods," but this leads to a strained interpretation of 35: "What is the meaning of these new concepts of the universe and the gods [i.e., the epiphany of the Muses just described] in contrast to the obscure, older beliefs [i.e., the oak and rock]?" The line is more likely to mean "what (or why) are these things to me concerning (or located around) the oak and rock" than "what are these things doing around the oak and rock." A local interpretation of περί (see above chapter 2 n. 3) would not materially affect either interpretation.

[65] The pattern was earlier applied by Friedländer 9 to the Muses.

[66] This is a fitting end to the whole *Theogony*, as several have argued, most recently Northrup 8f (see Appendix 3).

[67] I understand death as the ἕτερον κακόν of 602.

[68] West 44f, following Wade-Gery, sees here a reference to the death of Amphidamas, at whose funeral games Hesiod won a tripod which he dedicated to the Helikonian Muses (WD 654–59).

[69] Mazon (1928) 20. Schmid 262, Brown 11, Philippson 36 and Walcot (1966) 62 all sense the need for humans in the poem.

[70] Schwabl (1970) 452.


## NOTES TO CHAPTER FIVE

[1] Such "lyric narratives" are found in epic as well, see W. J. Slater, "Lyric Narrative: Structure and Principle," *CA* 2 (1983) 117–32.


## NOTES TO CHAPTER SIX

[1] By rough count 37 of the articles on Hesiod listed in *L'Année Philologique* from 1972 through 1985 were on the first part (25 on the two myths) and only 18 on the second part, mostly on a line or two. Critics ostensibly dealing with the whole poem tend to spend most of their time on the first part: Teggart's essay on the "argument" of the poem discusses only vv.1–382; Fuss likewise; Kerschensteiner devotes 36 pages to 1–382 and only 5 to the rest; Benardete 15 pages to the first part and 5 to the rest. Heath devotes less than half a page to the Calendar and over 5 to the first part. Verdenius's commentary goes only to 382.

[2] Usually translated "Strifes" but this is slightly misleading (strife is never good) so the Greek term will be used throughout.

[3] For surveys of the scholarship see Fuss 4–22 (to 1910), Jensen 1–3, Blusch 1–6 and especially Bona Quaglia 1–13.

[4] See e.g. Steitz, Susemihl, Aly. The "Liedertheorie," which divides the poem into a number of "songs," is in the same tradition.

[5] Wisdom poetry: Friedländer, F. Dornseiff, "Hesiods Werke und Tage und das alte Morgenland," *Philologus* 89 (1934) 397–415; paraenetic tradition: Diller; justice and work: see n.19 below. Other themes include Zeus (Kerchensteiner 190), truth (Bona Quaglia 20), the "moment juste"(van Groningen 297, Beye 37, Jones), and security (Blusch). Blusch 2 puts the change at 1910 but many proponents of the 'interpolation' school come later: Aly (1913), Diller (1962), Solmsen (1948, 1982).

[6] See Jensen 2 on Walcot; W. J. Verdenius *Mnemosyne* 30 (1977) 302–6 on Blusch; Bona Quaglia 11 ("una imposizione esterna") and Schwabl (1970) 464 on Nicolai. Recently Thalmann has revived some of Walcot's patterns, without much improvement, but he rightly stresses that the "basic principle of composition is the juxtaposing of discrete sections" (56).

[7] M. L. West in his review of Peabody, *Phoenix* 30 (1976) 385, concludes "I do not find any of this enlightening." Munding was widely criticized for asserting direct dependence on *our Iliad*. Nagy's idea of the beggar's quarrel was already developed by Peabody.

[8] Bona Quaglia 6 points to Waltz, Friedländer and Sellschopp, but the main proponents of the "associative" school come later: van Groningen, Verdenius, Beye, and S. Østerud, "The Individuality of Hesiod," *Hermes* 104 (1976) 14. West, too, is clearly in this tradition.

[9] See Nicolai 184f, Bona Quaglia 192f.

[10] West 46, approved by Renehan 341, Solmsen (1980) 210. Richardson 169 objects, "it does not explain why he chose to enlarge it in this way" and "I do not see why . . . lengthy premeditation cannot produce large-scale structural effects" but then adds "such . . . does not appear to be Hesiod's manner in this poem." See also Heath 247.

[11] Yet her act is clearly consonant with Zeus's plan, as the echo of ἐμήσατο κήδεα λυγρά 49 at 95 shows. Thalmann argues that the pithos story is fitted to the rest by ring structure but he openly omits the most obvious verbal echo (95 = 49).

[12] Both Jensen 15 and Verdenius 126 comment on how *bios* is passed over. Friedländer (1913) 562f, following Lisco, thought the absence looked toward the second part.

[13] Schmid 276, Walcot 5, Fränkel 120, Beye 35, Solmsen 83 n.27. See also West 174, Matthiessen 31.

[14] On the surprising absence of a proper moral see e.g. Fuss 44, Daly 48, Athanassakis 94. Peabody 253 argues that the hawk gives the moral: the nightingale has flown too high—not noting that it was the hawk who carried her there. Similarly Jensen 20–22 and V. A. Rodgers "Some Thoughts on ΔIKH," *CQ* 21 (1971) 290–92, effectively countered by M. W. Dickie, "*Dike* as a Moral Term in Homer and Hesiod," *CP* 73 (1978) 100f.

[15] Beginning with Kirchhoff (see West 35, whose position is not much different).

[16] West (53 n.2) remarks on the similar disruption of spring sailing (678ff).

[17] Nicolai 117.

[18] So e.g., Fuss 42, Mazon 69f, Kerschensteiner 171, Kumaniecki 81, Rosenmeyer 272ff, West 174; challenged by e.g. Smith 151f. See also Schwabl "Weltalter" *RE* Supp.15 col.795.

[19] So Fuss 45, Mazon (1928) 74, von Fritz (1962) 43, Sellschopp 120, Diller 63, Kumaniecki 84, van Groningen 285, Daly 49, Verdenius 138, Benardete 161, Schwabl 465, Solmsen (1980) 212 n.7, Heath 249. Bona Quaglia, on the other hand, argues (136) that since 275ff is addressed to Perses it cannot refer to the fable and she finds (145) that the echo is with good Eris: πολλὸν ἀρίστη 279 recalls πολλὸν ἀμείνω 19 (cf. ἄρισται 36). She does not note the closer echo in the fable (πολλὸν ἀρείων 207) and in 320 (πολλὸν ἀμείνω or the frequent occurrence of ἀρίστη(ν) in final position in the poem (471, 766, 781, 814, 820 cf. ἄριστος 585, 694, 719).

[20] "It is noticeable that the singer is coupled with the beggar" West 147.

[21] Mazon 56, Peabody 262 and Delgado 14 among others argue that v.45 predicts the Nautilia.

[22] In addition there are two animal ἀοιδοί: the nightingale in the fable (208, clearly representing Hesiod) and the cicada who sings at the height of summer (583).

[23] Thus we need not assume with West (273) that the wagon was meant to carry seed.

[24] This possibility is made even more tenuous by the fact that what is described is the gathering of wood for the wagon as opposed to the actual building of the plow. We later have

reference to building a wagon (455). One can find the same joining in 453 if, as West argues, this is a reference to plowing (but is it?).

[25] Nor is the poet/beggar pattern clear before the poetic competition is described. There Hesiod is first identified as a poet competing with poets. At that point one can look back and see the conflict between the brothers as poet vs. beggar.

[26] For example van Groningen 296 looks to vv.236, 247 rather than 45f for hints that the Nautilia is coming.

[27] The work "fails to live up to elementary standards of logic, consistency and structural coherence" (Barron 100).

[28] R. Harder *DLZ* 52 (1931) 495 notes that in both the *Works and Days* and the *Theogony* a statement about truth (WD 10, Th. 28) leads to the theme: "als im Prooemium der Theogonie das . . . neue Wahrheitsprogramm der Poesie aufgestellt ist, folgt, wie man es erwartet, alsbald auch der Inhalt dieser neuen Wahrheit, oder anders ausgedrückt, das Thema des Gedichts: Hymnos auf die ewigen Götter. Nicht anders steht es in den Erga . . . Die Lehre von den beiden Erides . . . ist der Inbegriff dieser neuen Wahrheit."

[29] ταῦτα then refers to all that precedes (so Nicolai 21f), not just good Eris (so West 148, Schmidt 29).

[30] A few critics have defined the Erides as the program, but without elaboration: Friedländer (1913) 563; E. Römisch *Studien zur älteren griechischen Elegie* (Frankfurt am Main, 1933) 43; E. Livrea, "I Proemio degli Erga considerato attraverso i vv.9–10," *Helikon* 6 (1966) 465. Others extend the "program" to 41, despite the ringing which clearly marks off the passage. So Fuss 32 interprets good Eris as (a) right work (16-26) and true justice (27–41) and sees these themes repeated in chiastic order after the myths: (b) 202–85; (a) 383ff, although he admits that 202–85 deals with bad Eris as well. Jensen, to be sure, divides the poem into evil Strife (27–285) and good Strife (286–828) but does not depend on 11–26 to define the sections and in fact is primarily interested in proving both parts refer to and are part of a court case. Rosenmeyer 262 says simply that the two Erides give "the ethical sights within which everything that follows is to be seen."

# NOTES TO CHAPTER SEVEN

[1] Nicolai identifies justice and work as the two "Programmpunkte" (167) and sees them both in both myths (168–70) and all parts of the poem (175). To his list of scholars concentrating on these two themes (164 n.2) add West 229, Bona Quaglia, Blusch 135, Fontenrose 12, and W. Liebermann, "Die Hälfte mehr als das Ganze," *Hermes* 109 (1981) 385–409. Blusch finds both work and justice in both parts of the poem, the difference being the first part is speculative while the second part deals with facts. He rejects the Erides as the theme (144).

[2] Solmsen 83 n.23 argues that πόνος 91 probably represents work since "in view of 42 . . . one might expect to find 'Work' (ἔργον) included among the evils." Yet in the *Theogony* (228) πόνος is the child of *bad* Eris.

[3] Susemihl 8 attacked the relevance of 11–26 precisely because there was no talk of the good Eris right away: "im folgenden . . . der Dichter auf die gute gar nicht ausdrücklich wieder zurückkommt" although he recognized the relationship between the good Eris and the second part of the poem: "hat der ganze Gedanke von dieser doppelten Eris nur Sinn durch die Beziehung auf das Ackerbaugedicht."

[4] West (181) comments that ἔργα in 119 "with its connotation of tillage, is not altogether apt." It may be significant that the Golden Age while living enjoys the absence of Pandora's evils and when dead enjoys the fruits of ἔργα. For the contrast between the Golden Age produce and farming see e.g. Plato's *Statesman* 272a5.

[5] The oak of the first part produces honey and acorns, typical golden age fare (cf Plato's *Republic* 372C, although Athanassakis 95 argues the acorns are for the farmer's animals), while the oak of the second part is cut down (I grant that it is a different oak, πρίνινον 429 vs. δρῦς 232).

[6] "The stories of a life of ease have nothing to do with us," Teggart 69. See also Matthiessen who argues (32) that the Heroic Age is meant to contrast with the present.

[7] West comments on 151: "Elsewhere in the poem . . . the verb refers to farm work, and Hesiod may be thinking of ploughshares and spades" but must admit this is inconsistent with 146.

[8] Kerchensteiner 149 uses "myth" and "reality" to describe the basic difference in content. Bona Quaglia speaks of the second part as "la vera descrizione della razza del ferro" (182) and notes that "in tutto questo quadro della vita dell'uomo laborioso non v'è ombra di pessimismo o di sfiducia nella giustizia" (183 n.46). Heath (248) on the other hand finds reference to work in Iron Age κάματος while admitting that the work-theme is minimal.

[9] This division was standard in 19th and early 20th C. criticism—see Fuss 4–22, Kerchensteiner 149f for lists. Nicolai's appendix 2 gives a helpful overview of how various critics divide the poem. Even those who divide the poem into many sections generally recognize an overriding two-part division.

[10] E.g. Fuss 28 n.3, van Groningen 283 n.2, Diller 51 n.19, Benardete 151, Walcot 2, Kumaniecki 80, West 142, Solmsen (1982) 7. Griffin 92, Schmidt 29. This is challenged by Delgado 11 n.9, who unconvincingly explains the imperfect as derived from "el valor de pasado implicito en γένος."

[11] See Benardete 152f and Bona Quaglia 37 for good remarks on the general differences between the two poems.

[12] As Fuss notes (36), we are hardly able to understand the *Works and Days* version without knowing the version given in the *Theogony* (although this does not mean we need that text, just that story).

[13] Teggart 49 calls it "the abridgement of a tale which had nothing to do with Prometheus or Pandora." Kerchensteiner 159 "eine neue Geschichte"; Kirk (1970) 230 "defective." C. J. Rowe, "'Archaic Thought' in Hesiod," *JHS* 103 (1983) 130, speaks of "two different, if overlapping, accounts."

[14] Thus Epimetheus' failure to heed his brother (οὐδ' Ἐπιμηθεύς / ἐφράσαθ' ὥς οἱ ἔειπε Προμηθεύς 85f) becomes the model for Hesiod's advice to Perses, to pay attention (φράζεσθαι 404, 448) and do as he orders (ὥς σε κελεύω 316, 536, 623, cf ὡς ἀγορεύω 688).

[15] Vernant (1977) 67f.

[16] Keeping WD 108 with West (vs. Solmsen).

[17] For Zeus's succession see West *ad* 111 and 143. Admittedly the two myths in the *Works and Days* do not mesh perfectly because of their role as independent and complete λόγοι. For the difficulty in fitting the details of the two myths together see Fontenrose 2. The most recent attempt is Kirk (1970) 228–38, not cited by Fontenrose.

[18] The fable is not a myth and is not part of the program; it is directed to the kings rather than Perseus, despite the statement in v.10 that Hesiod would be speaking to Perseus, and it has no analogue in the *Theogony*.

[19] The ἀνάγκη (15) that forces men to honor bad Eris does not reappear in the poem, but it does help define τιμή as that given by an inferior to a superior.

[20] So Nicolai 165, approved by Beye 35 n.32.

[21] "L'excellence du laboureur . . . s'oppose à l'excellence aristocratique du guerrier" Detienne 35. See also Solmsen 77.

[22] ὕβρις: 134, 146, 191, 213, 214, 217, 238; δίκη: 9, 36, 39, 124, 190, 192, 213, 217, 219, 220, 221, 225, 226, 239, 249, 250, 254, 256, 262, 264, 269, 270, 271, 272, 275, 278, 279, 280, 283. "δίκη nur in ganz bestimmten Partien der Erga auftritt," Schmidt 126. For the one exception (712) see below p. 751. Likewise war (πόλεμος: 14, 161, 229); strife (δῆρις: 14, 33); force (βίη: 148, 275, 321) occur mainly in the first part.

[23] Only in the first part is Zeus "il protagonista," Bona Quaglia 180. "Zeus now appears

not as the father of Justice but the god of the sky," Benardete 165.

²⁴ We find occurrences of undifferentiated θεός frequently in the first part (42, 59, 62, 73, 80, 85, 108, 112, 120, 139, 178, 187, 251, 257) and in the two sets of injunctions surrounding the Calendar (289, 303, 325, 336, 741, 742, 756, 764) but not in the Calendar or Days (except 398).

²⁵ Contrast the Golden Age with its γέρας βασιλήιον (126).

²⁶ With the exception of one cluster (354–58) gifts, too, drop out after the first part: "gift-eaters" (39, 221, 264, ringing the first part); Pandora (57, 82, 85, 86); gods' gift (178) then only 614, a periphrasis for wine ("Dionysus' gift").

²⁷ For φυτεύειν see West 146.

²⁸ Alternatively one may understand the relative clause (ὅς . . . θέσθαι 22f) as defining the actions of the one seeing the wealthy man. Such an interpretation would provide a clearer model for Perses, who now spends his time gazing at (ὀπιπεύοντ᾽ 29) court cases and not working at all.

²⁹ The contrast is neatly paralleled in the description of the Cyclopes in the *Odyssey*:

θεοῖσι πεποιθότες ἀθανάτοισιν
οὔτε φυτεύουσιν χερσὶν φυτὸν οὔτ᾽ ἀρόωσιν (9.108–9).

³⁰ For diligence and forethought see e.g. Blusch 148–51, Jones.

³¹ Demeter occurs at structurally significant points: at the beginning of the first part (32), the beginning of the second part (300) and the beginning of the Almanac (393).

³² Cf Od.17.382–85, where Odysseus' list of itinerant craftsmen (with whom the beggar must compete) comprises seers, doctors, shipbuilders and singers.

³³ Matched by the νόμος established by Zeus for animals (276) to eat each other, which fuses the two meanings, "custom" (νόμος) and "feeding" (νομός, as in 526). We should hear "tune" (νόμος) as well as "range" (νομός in 403, opposing beggar and poet.

³⁴ "A strife between bards," Peabody 246 (and nn.82, 84); on 266 he again suggests that both men are singers. For criticism of Munding's somewhat similar view, see Diller 46. A parallel that should be discussed in this regard is Dicaeopolis in *Acharnians*, who borrows a beggar's outfit from Euripides so he can become a poet. In discussing v.26, Fränkel 115 n.1 already compared the jealousy between beggars in *Odyssey* 18, remarking that singers are not much better off than beggars.

³⁵ Bona Quaglia 186 speaks of a "vittoria non bellica, ma poetica."

³⁶ So West 232, but see Renehan 351. I cannot imagine why Peabody 485 n.76 thinks Paris was called δῖον γένος. Nagy 64 argues that Perses "formalizes the negative side of what Zeus does to those marked by *hubris*" and so is called of Zeus's race. An even more remote possibility is that this reflects the genealogy of the Persians as children of Perseus and Andromeda (Herodotus 7.61.3), thereby making Perses the original example of both savagery and luxury.

³⁷ I realize that I am treading on dangerous ground here, especially since πρός meaning "descended from," though common later, is not found in Homer. Still the choices for the not common epic use of πρός with the genitive seem to be: (a) "(swear) by/in the name of"; (b) "(done) by"; (c) "coming from" (local); (d) "coming from/belonging to." This last (which seems to be used only once, *Iliad* 1.239, describing laws from Zeus) seems the only reasonable choice for our beggars.

³⁸ In fact anger (κότος) and envy (φθόνος) are not mentioned again. ζῆλος, on the other hand, is mentioned again in 195 and 312, the former linked by its epithet κακόχαρτος with the bad Eris (28). "The good Eris is accompanied by a good Zelos (23, 312)" West 203.

³⁹ Although νήπιος is used frequently (40, 131, 218, 456), it is used of Perses only in 286, 397, where he is a beggar, and 633.

⁴⁰ The ἐσθλά that Hesiod will tell Perses (286) recall the ἐτήτυμα that he will tell him in the proem (10).

⁴¹ I find myself anticipated in this by Jensen 24f, Peabody 493 n.92 and Schmidt 48f, who note many of the parallels. Friedländer 567 n.1 had noted the echo of 34 at 315, Kerschensteiner 184f the echo of 6 at 325. See also Bona Quaglia, who, however, does not draw the same

conclusion about structure: "il cerchio del ragionamento iniziato al v.11 si sta chiaramente chiudendo" (146). Likewise Thalmann 57.

[42] West 40, followed by Griffin 95. This is not to say, with some, that Perses may be a poetic construct (already Fuss 25; see also Nagy 64f). Nagy (59) argues that Perses' different roles reflect "the passage of time required for the worship of Dike": the kings are eventually disqualified, and "it is as if Perses were now tacitly ready to accept the teachings of his righteous brother." See also Griffith 59, Jones 319f and, in opposition, Schmidt 50f. One might add that the Nautilia shows that Perses now has sufficient property to engage in trade (West 40, challenged by Schmidt 51). But if we reduce all the injunctions to personal history we will soon be in trouble. For example, Mazon (140) assumed that the injunctions in 695ff suggest that Perses is ready to get married, but we know from 399 that he already has a wife and children. There are really only the two places where Perses' situation is described.

[43] So Kumaniecki 92, "the three appeals follow the three narratives." Likewise Schwabl 465, except that, looking simply at the vocatives, he finds four parts. Bona Quaglia 142 extends the third section from 274 to 382.

[44] Thus this is not "a mere dribble of additional thoughts" (West 50).

[45] For a list of repetitions see appendix 4. A similar argument on the basis of these lines is made by von Fritz (1962) 42. For defense of the lines see Matthiessen 26 n.6, Jensen 17 and Verdenius (1985) 86f.

[46] The only other occurrence of ὄπις is 706, which marks the reversal effected by the end of the poem.

[47] Virginity is shown by the white dress of Aidos, "suggesting modesty and purity" (West 203).

[48] Also we have echoes of Hesiod's legal dispute in the first set of imperatives (δωροφάγοι 221 = 39, though in 221 they are not specified as kings) as well as in the second set (the δωροφάγοι kings need straight justice 263f, cf. 36ff).

[49] Fuss notes of the Ages myth that "der Hauptpunkt der ganzen Erzählung bleibt wiederum unerwähnt" (41). So Jensen 16, Smith 151.

[50] "The moral simply does not suit Hesiod's purpose" (Daly 46).

[51] For a full discussion of the imperatives see Bona Quaglia 142–44, who argues for an elaborate chiasmus: (a) work (Erides, Prometheus myth); (b) justice (Ages myth. addressed to Perses; fable to the kings); (b) justice (213–47 to Perses; 248–73 to the kings); (a) work (274–382). This ignores the fact that 274–382 is not concerned only with work.

[52] West (213) is extreme in arguing that the description of the just city "contradicts the myth" of the Ages.

[53] Similarly West 226. The ταῦτα in 27 and 274 is emphatic and distinguishes these commands to Perses from other more limited ones such as 213, 299, 397, 611, 641.

[54] Unless we wish to argue that the chiastic order (rudder, work of ox, work of ox, rudder) is noticeable—but even here the initial order is not illogical (contrast the chiasmus of wagon/plow discussed above).

[55] "Optional supplement," West 313, followed by Jones 310 n.8.

[56] "The premise is now . . . that he [Perses] has surplus grain (βίον 689, cf. 601) to sell abroad," West 40.

[57] For the alternate times for plowing and sailing see Nicolai 126.

[58] As Steitz 152 noted, Boeotia is poorly situated for sea trade.

## NOTES TO CHAPTER EIGHT

[1] West 55f, followed by Solmsen (1982) 30.

[2] For some interesting speculation on truth, memory and the Muses see Detienne 41–48.

³Peabody 262 notes that 650–59 echoes the "contest challenge" of 36–40. Thalmann 23 discusses the contrast between Hesiod and his father.

⁴This is the Homeric epithet for Greece not Troy: "Hesiod's choice of epithets in this line is remarkable," Edwards 80.

⁵θάλασσα is mentioned only twice elsewhere in the poem and in both cases merely as part of a general whole: earth and sea (101), those who dwell on the plain and those near the sea (388).

⁶Richardson 170 mentions the possibility that the funeral games of Amphidamas are modelled on the *Iliad*, where an Amphidamas occurs in close proximity to Patroklos' funeral games (23.87). West (321) argues that the influence was the reverse.

⁷Note that the only metals mentioned after 286 are bronze and iron.

⁸Actually Hesiod says he would rather have died in the Heroic Age. This may confirm my point about the impossibility of the heroic paradise.

⁹Benardete 156 equates just city with Golden Age and just Iron Age with Heroic. See also Solmsen 87.

¹⁰So West (191) comments on death in the Heroic Age, "it is exactly the same as that of the Bronze race: they killed each other off." There was no seafaring in the Golden Age; see R. Scodel, "The Achaean Wall and the Myth of Destruction," *HSCP* 86 (1982) 49. Hesiod as poet "transcends the realm of scarcity and work," Benardete 163.

¹¹If West is correct to interpret μείναντες χειμῶνα (652) as "waiting until winter (was over)," the most we can say is that they gathered as if to sail during the winter. But West's is a strange interpretation of μένειν given 674.

¹²Does the Homeric first part yield to the Hesiodic second part? Hesiod was no "war poet," G. Nussbaum, "Labour and Status in the *Works and Days*," *CQ* 10 (1960) 217, following Wade-Gary. M. Puelma notes that the hawk in the fable sounds like a Homeric warrior, "Sanger und Konig," *MH* 29 (1972) 89.

¹³Though Steitz 146f, for example, makes the order depend on crops.

¹⁴Perses may beg successfully two or three times at best (401) just as he was successful in court once but will not be a second time (34).

¹⁵Contrast Demeter who fills one's καλιή (301, 307). The only other occurrence of the term is 374, where the Pandoralike woman seeks one's καλιή, and as we will see below there is a close connection between Pandora and idle talk based on hope.

¹⁶We should remember that in the *Odyssey* (18.327) this is where the beggar will go for shelter—not that Hesiod's audience need recognize the specific passage but only the idea embedded in the tradition.

¹⁷West is really speaking about the Lenaion section (504–63), which has long been considered an insert (e.g. Schmid 277; cf. Walcot 9f). The Winter section actually begins at 493.

¹⁸See West 53.

¹⁹We should note how the epithet "ox-flaying" (βουδόρα 504) is realized first in the "mooing" winds (508) blowing through the ox's hide (515) and then in the clothing made from the skin of the slaughtered ox (541, 544).

²⁰This answers in part West's question (258), "why is Hesiod so emphatic?" γυμνός may mean "stripped" not "naked" (see *Clouds* 498, *Lysistrata* 1020, *Republic* 474a).

²¹The inclusive nature of the reference to the Pleiades, clear from the reference to both their appearance and disappearance περιπλομένου ἐνιαυτοῦ (386) is reinforced by the command to be stripped both for sowing and for reaping (391f). In addition, West (256) notes the inclusive but technically inappropriate formula νύκτας τε καὶ ἤματα in 385. Finally, the Pleiades do *not* rise when the iron (scythe) is being sharpened as Hesiod says in 387 but rather the reverse, and this mild grammatical dissonance is corrected in 573.

²²Arktouros and the Pleiades form a pattern in this section: Arktouros (566) with grapes, Pleiades (572) with grain then Arktouros (610) with grapes followed by the Pleiades (615) with grain. See Nicolai 208 for an even more elaborate arrangement.

²³E.g. Schwabl (1970) 469, Nicolai 89.

[24] The centrality of the Lenaion section is marked by the mention of animals and wheels both before and after it.

[25] A further possible contrast is between Pandora being dressed by the gods and making one's own clothes for winter, but there are no verbal echoes. The contrast between Pandora and winter maiden may inform Sophocles' *Trachiniae* 144–47 as well.

[26] My sensible editor refuses to let me connect the idle talk at the χαλκεῖον θῶκον (493) and Hesiod's trip to Χαλκίς (655) for a singing contest. Even unfettered, I would not go so far as to say that Hesiod traveled from Courtyard (Aulis) to Bronze Place (Chalkis) in Good Cow (Euboia) or that his father traveled from Wave in Wind (Aeolic Kyme) to Bare Oak (Ascra), though some might.

[27] Nicolai 171, "etwas ausserhalb der beiden Programmspunkte; Benardete 165, "a precious interlude." See also West 45. The opening of the second part is further complicated by a short extension of the introduction that harks back to the justice theme: Nicolai even makes a separate Dike parainesis of 320–41, although the echo of the poem's opening argues against that.

[28] See e.g. Mazon 142, Walcot 8, van Groningen 287, Benardete 167, Schwabl (1970) 468.

[29] Kerchensteiner 185 and Bona Quaglia 193 connect the first set of injunctions and the Iron Age and we have seen (above Chapter 6 n.46) with ὄπις that it is connected with the second set as well.

[30] This is less true of the second set of injunctions.

[31] Walcot (1966) 83; Diller 69; Nicolai 143. Bona Quaglia has shown at length (218–22) how fame is a major theme of the second set of imperatives and how 760–64 recalls the proem.

[32] The two vocatives to Perses (286, 299) mark a two-fold introduction to the second part. See Delgado 11.

[33] τῶν μέν in 335 summarizes and so is structurally important, like ταῦτα in 27 and 274 (see above Chapter 6 n.53).

[34] Keeping 370–72 with Verdenius (1985) 176f.

[35] Renehan 353 criticizes West and follows the usual interpretation of ἕτερον παῖδ' in 378 as "second son" (see Bona Quaglia 211 n.38 for a full discussion). So Richardson 170, who notes "the relevance of these lines to Hesiod's own situation may be worth considering" (following the scholiast). Kumaniecki 85 thinks Perses had several sons! Sellschopp 114 discusses the connection of 342–82 with Perses' situation in 397ff.

[36] The burning of μηρία (337) may look to Mekone.

[37] ἐξαπατάω occurs only in 48, 323 and 373.

[38] αἱμύλος occurs only in 78, 374 and 789.

[39] Thus we need not say, with Kirk (1970) 231, that Pandora's deceit "is not particularly germane." Note also the pun on φιλοῖς in φιλήτῃσιν 375.

[40] I wonder if the "curious use" (Richardson 171) of ληΐζεται (702) for obtaining one's wife is meant to contrast with the warlike first part or simply reflects 'bride-rape.'

[41] Van Groningen 286 was wrong to complain that "aucune de ces recommandations ne présente le moindre rapport avec la situation spéciale."

[42] For a similar analysis see Thalmann 203 n.68.

## NOTES TO CHAPTER NINE

[1] The list of those attacking the Days is long, see Bona Quaglia 229 n.1 and add Jimenez, Roesch, Heath. Some continue to defend the whole: Detienne 43 thinks the religious aspect is central to Hesiod's work; Jensen 27 argues the Days are a "piece of esoteric knowledge," the "climax" of 724–59. See also Walcot (1966) 99–102.

[2] See above Chapter 7 n.31. The idea is criticized by van Groningen 290.

³One might argue that the farmer turned sailor is being subtly told to avoid sailing entirely, much as the Nautilia tries very hard to discourage it. The other difficulties raised by Solmsen 296 can be explained differently: woodcutting, to be done "when the might of the sun's heat ceases and Sirius is overhead briefly" (414–19), can easily be fitted to the specification of the seventeenth as the day to cut wood (805). The servants should be ordered to thresh in the well-rounded threshing floor when Orion first appears (597f) and to "throw" the grain in the well-rounded threshing floor on the seventeenth. Solmsen complains that the farmer may have to wait as much as twenty-eight or twenty-nine days after the rising of Orion on a given year, but this makes no distinction between threshing and winnowing.

⁴Roesch argues that there is almost perfect overlap between farming advice and forward-numbered days whereas the other numbering systems are primarily involved with lucky and unlucky days and that Boeotian calendars used forward-numbering. There are problems with both arguments. The Boeotian calendars are much later than Hesiod and may be influenced by him. Also, there are many more exceptions to Roesch's rule than he notes: we find both forward-numbered days that do not have to do with farming (the 12th for weaving, the 4th for getting married and building a boat, the 10th for producing males) and other days that do (first 6th for gelding animals and building pens, the middle 4th for taming animals).

⁵The "old" day (ἔνη) is a bit confusing and is usually understood as a shortened form of the "old and new" day (ἔνη καὶ νέα) but ἔνη "occasionally stands by itself for the 30th" (West 351) and this is the way we should understand it here. The explanatory (γάρ) clause confirms this assumption: the thirtieth (τριηκάδα 766) is best for overseeing work and dividing produce *because* it (i.e., ἔνη 770) is one of the "days from Zeus."

⁶West's crucial repunctuation of 772 is guaranteed by the particles.

⁷These are good days (see West 358f) and so not in contradiction to 819–21, as Roesch, most recently, has argued.

⁸I interpret "thrice-ninth" as Hesiod's way of specifying as unambiguously as possible the "last ninth" as the 29th, since in some systems the "last ninth" could be the 22nd. So Roesch (31), who concludes "le poète joue ici sur le chiffre 'neuf.'"

⁹The traditional reading of 819–21, as presented in the OCT, is therefore preferable to West's alteration. West finds the two elipses in 820 difficult (μέσση for μέσση τετράς and μέτ' εἰκάδα for τὴν μέτ' εἰκάδα τετράδα), but his only argument is that elsewhere μέσση has its noun expressed—as it must since elsewhere it is always the first date (and sometimes the only date); here however the noun has already been expressed and so supplying it is not at all difficult, and most editors have not had trouble with it. Once again, Hesiod seems to be making sure we understand what is meant by the "last fourth." Here again, as with the "last ninth" the Argive system is meant, so that the last fourth is the 24th not the 26th.

¹⁰It is worth considering the possibility that behind σπέρματος . . . φυτά Hesiod is thinking of children. Certainly, he goes on to talk about children, not crops, and in the second part he seems to use φυτευέμεν of children (812).

¹¹The equation of Pandora = Woman is clear from the *Theogony*: "the version of the *Theogony* has so strong a hold on Hesiod's mind that . . . woman herself seems to be the κακόν intended for mankind," Solmsen (1980) 213.

¹²371 should be kept (so Verdenius 146, Nicolai 85).

¹³So already Sellschopp 114, rejected by West 249.

¹⁴406 complicates 405: "why should Hesiod be concerned to replace the wife by a slave-woman who does not feature in the rest of the poem?" (West 260). This complication is worked out in the course of the poem: at the end of the Almanac (602f) we hear of acquiring a childless slave-woman and then of marrying a suitable virgin (699). We might note, finally, that 405 has no verb—perhaps because Perses is not able to afford a house or ox and already has a wife.

¹⁵789 echoes 78; Pandora's evil ways have become male. West 356, who calls them "positive qualities," says this is because it is Hermes' day.

¹⁶φυτεύειν (812) does not mean simply "plant."

¹⁷See Benardete 166, who notes that this actually starts at 502 (see also 573, 597).

[18] The halfway point is marked by 346 where a bad neighbor is a πῆμα (like Pandora 56, 82) but a good one a μέγ' ὄνειαρ. These are the only occurrences of ὄνειαρ in the poem.

[19] See Bona Quaglia chapter 6.

[20] So Jimenez 118, citing Mazon; vs. Solmsen (1963).

[21] This idea is generally mentioned only to be rejected, e.g., by P. Walcot *CR* 15 (1965) 160 and Diller 42 n.5.

[22] "After six lines defining the season, only the briefest word of what to do" (West 301). See also Heath 255.

[23] For the only other occurrence of πόλις see above p. 58. For οἶκος also see above p. 58.

## NOTES TO CHAPTER TEN

[1] So Jensen 2, criticizing Walcot, "as such resemblances or repetitions occur so frequently, analyses of this kind become extremely subjective, or even misleading."

[2] E.g. Sellschopp, Nicolai.

[3] F. Krafft, *Vergleichende Untersuchungen zu Homer und Hesiod*, Göttingen, 1963.

[4] See appendix 4 for details.

## NOTES TO THE APPENDICES

[1] E. Siegmann, "Χίμαιρα, Hesiod Theog. 319," *Hermes* 96 (1968) 755–57.

[2] This at first appears to be false: Keto produces Medusa who produces Chrysaor who produces Geryon and so we are the third generation from Keto. But Hesiod quite clearly says that Chrysaor and Pegasus "leapt out" from the decapitated Medusa and that implies that they are full-grown and so the chronology can be saved. It should be noted that Pegasus is later connected with Medusa's sister Chimera not her cousins and that Heracles as great-grandson of Ouranos is appropriately faced with great-grandchildren of Pontos.

[3] H. Schwabl, "Aufbau und Genealogie des hesiodischen Ungeheuerkatalogs," *Glotta* 47 (1970) 174–84. Marg 163ff, apparently knowing only West's arguments and not even considering Keto as a possibility, thought Echidna the mother of Chimera, Phix and the Nemean lion.

[4] He contradicts this later (178) when he does *not* take the immediately preceding female as the referent for ἡ δέ in 319.

[5] C. Robert, "Pandora," *Hermes* 49 (1914) 33 n. 2. See also Marg 237.

[6] Verdenius (1971) 6 cites with approval Fink's suggestion that the plurality of her crowns is simply to magnify her beauty.

[7] See also Schwenn 132 n. 3. There are problems with most of these arguments: Sellschopp depends on an arbitrary dating of the Homeric hymns and ignores the *Works and Days* (see Verdenius [1971] p. 6); Lendle's conclusion is patently absurd.

[8] See T. McEvilley, "Sapphic Imagery and Fragment 96," *Hermes* 101 (1973) 266.

[9] See e.g. N. J. Richardson *The Homeric Hymn to Demeter* (Oxford 1974) 140.

[10] See now P. Smith, *Nursling of Mortality* (Frankfurt a.M. 1981) 41.

[11] Neitzel 22ff also defends both crowns but interprets the flowers as a sort of earring (!), reading παρέθηκε in 577 with the mss. M. Blech *Studien zur Kranz bei der Griechen RGVV* 38 (Berlin 1982) 34 has no problem with both crowns which he distinguishes linguistically, στέφανος normally referring to flower chaplets and στεφάνη to more monumental, metal diadems. Yet a quick look at *LSJ* will show this distinction is not absolute.

[12] London E 467 (ARV² 601.23), conveniently illustrated in A. W. Pickard-Cambridge, *Dithyramb, Tragedy and Comedy* (Oxford 1962²) plate XVa, and his *The Dramatic Festivals of Athens* (Oxford 1968²) fig. 42.

[13] C. H. Smith *Catalogue of the Greek and Etruscan Vases in the British Museum* (London 1896) vol. 3 p. 285.

[14] See types AIa and AIb in A. Krug, *Binden in der griechischen Kunst* (Hösel, 1968). For spotted crowns by the same painter see T. B. L. Webster *Der Niobidenmaler* (Leipzig 1935) fig. 8a, 9a, 11a. It may legitimately be objected that the Niobid painter often shows crowns without such ties.

[15] Schwabl 137 grants that "Man wird die exakte Entsprechung der Verszahl nicht pressen," but this eliminates his strongest point. The other transition 963–68 also causes him trouble: he needs to begin counting at 965 to preserve his arithmetical balance between 938–64, 965–91, and 992–1018 (each 27 lines) but needs to consider 969 a beginning ("die Liste der Göttinnen, die sich Sterblichen verbanden, setzt 969 ein" 132) to have the pattern Zeus (886), Demeter (912), Zeus (938), Demeter (969). One hunts in vain for a justification of the break at 992.

[16] Aphrodite occurs a number of other places (975, 980, 1005) that are not fitted into his pattern.

[17] F. Brommer *Vasenlisten zur griechischen Heldensage* (Marburg 1973³) 159–74.

[18] See D. L. Page, *The Homeric Odyssey* (Oxford 1955) 25 and nn.6,7. Northrup 12 n.10 concludes, "no one knows for certain where or when Heracles was first accorded divine status."

[19] See also Marg 293.

[20] A point often made, most recently by Northrup 11 n.4.

[21] Some may wish to use the only other early occurrence of "wife" (410, the wife of Perses) as evidence for West's theory about Hesiod the evangelist of Hecate.

[22] One might note that these examples are all in the doubtful portion.

[23] He makes a third point, that thematically the material is foreign to the *Theogony*, but this suffers from the same circularity as West's contention that Heracles is not a god in epic.

[24] Schwabl's problems (1970) 445 include: Eris, Pontos, Thaumas, Hyperion, Krios, and Krios's children.

[25] Contrast the Nereids: Pontos produces children either without a mate, or without love, and these children either go outside their family for a mate (Nereus, Thaumas) or produce monsters (Phorcys and Keto), who dominate the male (Typhaon, Orthos).

[26] Hermes resembles Pan in 444, as guardian of flocks; contrast his absence in the *Theogony* version of the Prometheus story with his presence in the *Works and Days* version.

[27] See already Schoemann (272), "es bleib also nur Poseidon übrig."

[28] Ziegler (1493) defends it: "es wäre sonst der einzige Titanenspross, dessen Deszendenz ungenannt bleibe" (which does not explain its odd position). West sees it as preparation "for the following paragraphs about them" (419; so Schwabl 130ff).

# BIBLIOGRAPHY

W. Aly, "Hesiodos von Askra und der Verfasser der Theogonie," *RhM* 68 (1913) 22–67 ( = Heitsch 50–99).

M. B. Arthur, "The Dream of a World Without Women: Poetics and Circles of Order in the *Theogony* Prooemium," *Arethusa* 16 (1983) 97–116.

A. N. Athanassakis, *Hesiod*, Baltimore, 1983.

J. P. Barron and P. E. Easterling, "Hesiod," in *The Cambridge History of Classical Literature* I (Cambridge 1985) 92–105.

S. Benardete, "Hesiod's *Works and Days*: A First Reading," *Agon* 1 (1967) 150–74.

C. R. Beye, "The Rhythm of Hesiod's *Works and Days*," *HSCP* 76 (1972) 23–43.

J. Blusch, *Formen und Inhalt von Hesiods Individuellem Denken*, Bonn, 1970.

L. Bona Quaglia, *Gli "Erga" di Esiodo*, Turin, 1973.

E. M. Bradley, "The Relevance of the Prooemium to the Design and Meaning of Hesiod's *Theogony*," *SO* 41 (1966) 29–47.

E. M. Bradley (1969), "*Theogony* 35," *SO* 44 (1969) 7–22.

N. O. Brown, *Hesiod Theogony*, Indianapolis, 1953.

L. W. Daly, "Hesiod's Fable," *TAPA* 92 (1961) 45–51.

J. A. Fernández Delgado, "Sobre forma y contenido de 'Los Trabajos y los Dias,'" in *Estudios de Forma y Contenido sobre los Generos Literarios Griegos* (Caceres 1982) 9–29.

M. Detienne, *Crise agraire et attitude religieuse chez Hésiode*, Brussels, 1963.

H. Diller, "Die dichterische Form von Hesiods Erga," *Abhandlungen der Ak.d.Wiss. Mainz* 1962 #2, 41–69 ( = Heitsch 239–74).

G. P. Edwards, *The Language of Hesiod in its Traditional Context*, Oxford, 1971.

J. Fontenrose, "Work, Justice, and Hesiod's Five Ages," *CP* 69 (1974) 1–16.

H. Frankel, *Early Greek Poetry and Philosophy*, New York, 1975.

P. Friedländer (1913), "ΥΠΟΘΗΚΑΙ," *Hermes* 48 (1913) 558–616. ( = Heitsch 223–38).

P. Friedländer, "Das Proömium von Hesiods Theogonie," *Hermes* 49 (1914) 1–16 ( = Heitsch 277–94).

K. von Fritz, "Das Proömium der hesiodischen Theogonie," *Festschrift Bruno Snell* (Munich 1956) 29–45 ( = Heitsch 295–315).

K. von Fritz (1962), "Das Hesiodische in den Werken Hesiods" *Entretiens sur l'antiquité classique* VII (Geneva 1962) 1–60.

W. Fuss, *Versuch einer Analyse von Hesiods ΕΡΓΑ ΚΑΙ ΗΜΕΡΑΙ*, Leipzig 1910.

J. Griffin, "Greek Myth and Hesiod," in *The Oxford History of the Classical World* (Oxford 1986) 78–98.

M. Griffith, "Personality in Hesiod," *CA* 2 (1983) 37–65.

B. A. van Groningen, *La Composition litéraire archaïque grecque*, Amsterdam, 1958.

M. Heath, "Hesiod's Didactic Poetry," *CQ* 35 (1985) 245–63.

E. Heitsch, *Hesiod*, Darmstadt, 1966.

R. Janko, "The Structure of the Homeric Hymns. A Study of Genre," *Hermes* 109 (1981) 9–22.

M. S. Jensen, "Tradition and Individuality in Hesiod's Works and Days," *C&M* 27 (1966) 1–27.

A. P. Jiménez, "Los "Días" de Hesiódo: Estructura Formal Y Analisis de Contenido," *Emerita* (1977) 105–23.

N. F. Jones, "Perses, Work 'in Season,' and the Purpose of Hesiod's *Works and Days*, *CJ* 79 (1984) 307–23.

A. Kambylis, *Die Dichterweihe und ihre Symbolik*, Heidelberg, 1965.

J. Kerschensteiner, "Zu Aufbau und Gedankenfuhrung von Hesiods Erga," *Hermes* 79 (1944) 149–91.

G. S. Kirk, "The Structure and Aim of the *Theogony*," *Entretiens sur l'antiquité classique* VII (Geneva 1962).

G. S. Kirk (1970), *Myth*, Berkeley, 1970.

T. Kraus, *Hekate*, Heidelberg, 1960.

K. Kumaniecki, "The Structure of Hesiod's *Works and Days*," *BICS* 10 (1963) 79–96.

D. Lemke, "Sprachliche und strukturelle Beobachtungen zum Ungeheuerkatalog in der Theogonie Hesiods," *Glotta* 46 (1968) 47–53.

O. Lendle, *Die "Pandorasage" bei Hesiod*, Würzburg, 1957.

H. Maehler, *Die Auffassung des Dichterberufs im frühen Griechentum bis zur Zeit Pindar*, Göttingen, 1963.

W. Marg, *Hesiod Sämtliche Gedichte*, Zurich, 1970.

P. A. Marquandt, "The Two Faces of Hesiod's Muse," *ICS* 7 (1982) 1–12.

K. Matthiessen, "Form und Funktion des Weltaltermythos bei Hesiod," *Arktouros* ed. G. W. Bowersock (Berlin 1979) 25–32.

P. Mazon, *Hesiode: Les Travaux et les Jours*, Paris, 1914.

P. Mazon (1928), *Hesiode*, Paris, 1928.

W. W. Minton, "The Proem-Hymn of Hesiod's *Theogony*," *TAPA* 101 (1970) 357–77.

R. Mondi, "The Ascension of Zeus and the Composition of Hesiod's *Theogony*," *GRBS* 25 (1984) 325–44.

G. Nagy, "Hesiod," *Ancient Writers* ed. T. J. Luce (New York 1982) 43–73.

H. Neitzel, *Homer-Rezeption bei Hesiod*, Bonn, 1975.

W. Nicolai, *Hesiods Erga*, Heidelberg, 1964.

M. D. Northrup, "Where did the *Theogony* End?" *SO* 58 (1983) 7–13.

B. Peabody, *The Winged Word*, Albany, 1975.

F. Pfister, "Die Hekate-Episode in Hesiods Theogonie," *Philologus* 84 (1929) 1–9.

P. Philippson, *Genealogie als mythische Form*, Oslo, 1936 (= Heitsch 651–87).

F. C. Philips Jr., "Narrative Compression and the Myths of Prometheus in Hesiod," *CJ* 68 (1973) 289–305.

R. Renehan, "Progress in Hesiod," *CP* 75 (1980) 339–58.

N. J. Richardson, rev. West *Hesiod Works and Days*, *JHS* 99 (1979) 169–71.

P. Roesch, "Le Calendrier d'Hesiode," ΣΤΗΛΗ (Festschrift Kontoleon) ed. B. K. Lambinoudakes (Athens 1980) 26–32.

T. J. Rosenmeyer, "Hesiod and Historiography," *Hermes* 85 (1957) 257–85.

S. Said, "Les Combats de Zeus," *REG* 90 (1977) 183–210.

A. E. Samuel, "The Days of 'Hesiod's' Month," *TAPA* 97 (1966) 421–30.

W. Schmid, *Geschichte der griechischen Literatur* vol.1 part 1, Munich, 1929.

J.-U. Schmidt, *Adressat und Paraineseform*, Göttingen, 1986.

G. F. Schoemann, *Die Hesiodische Theogonie*, Berlin, 1868.

H. Schwabl, *Hesiods Theogonie*, Vienna, 1966.

H. Schwabl (1970), "Hesiod," *Pauly-Wissowa* (*RE*) Supplementband 12 (Stuttgart 1970) 434–86.

F. Schwenn, *Die Theogonie des Hesiodos*, Heidelberg, 1934.

I. Sellschopp, *Stilistische Untersuchungen zu Hesiod*, Hamburg, 1934.

E. Siegmann, "Zu Hesiods Theogonieproömium," Festschrift E. Kapp (Hamburg 1958) 9–14 (= Heitsch 316–23).

P. Smith, "History and the Individual in Hesiod's Myth of Five Races," *CW* 74 (1980) 145–63.

F. Solmsen, *Hesiod and Aeschylus*, Ithaca, 1949.

F. Solmsen (1963), "The 'Days' of the *Works and Days*," *TAPA* 94 (1963) 293–320.

F. Solmsen (1980), rev. West *Hesiod Works and Days*, *Gnomon* 52 (1980) 209–21.

F. Solmsen (1982), "The Earliest Stages in the History of Hesiod's Text," *HSCP* 86 (1982) 1–31.

A. Steitz, *Die Werke und Tage des Hesiodos*, Leipzig, 1869.

F. Susemihl, "Zur Literatur des Hesiodos," *Jahrb. f.cl. Phil.* 10 (1864) 1–10, 729–53 (= Heitsch 3–49).

J. Svenbro, *La Parole et le Marbre: aux origines de la poétique grecque*, Lund, 1976.

F. J. Teggart, "The Argument of Hesiod's *Works and Days*," *JHI* 8 (1947) 45–77.

W. G. Thalmann, *Conventions of Form and Thought in Early Greek Epic Poetry*, Baltimore 1984.

W. J. Verdenius, "Aufbau und Absicht der Erga," *Entretiens sur l'antiquité classique* VII (Geneva 1962) 109–70.

W. J. Verdenius (1971), "Hesiod, *Theogony* 507–616," *Mnemosyne* 24 (1971) 1–10.

W. J. Verdenius (1972), "Notes on the Proem of Hesiod's *Theogony*," *Mnemosyne* 25 (1972) 225–60.

W. J. Verdenius (1985), *A Commentary on Hesiod Works and Days vv.1–382*, Leiden, 1985.

J. P. Vernant, "Mètis et les mythes de souveraineté," *RHR* 180 (1971) 29–76.

15. J. P. Vernant (1977), "Sacrifical and alimentary codes in Hesiod's Myth of Prometheus," in R. L. Gordon, *Myth, Religion and Society* (Cambridge 1981) 57–79 (first published as "Sacrifice et alimentation humaine à propos du Promethée d'Hésiode," *ASNP* 7 [1977] 905–40).

P. Walcot, "The Composition of the *Works and Days*," *REG* 74 (1961) 1–19.

P. Walcot (1966), *Hesiod and the Near East*, Cardiff, 1966.

M. L. West, *Hesiod Theogony*, Oxford, 1966.

M. L. West, *Hesiod Works and Days*, Oxford, 1978.

U. von Wilamowitz-Moellendorff, *Hesiods Erga*, Berlin, 1928.

K. Ziegler, "Theogonien," *Roscher's Lexicon* (Leipzig 1916–24) vol.5, 1469–1554.

# INDEX OF WORKS AND PASSAGES

Aeschylus: *Choephoroi 585ff*, 94, 112; *Prometheus*, 34, 109; *7*, 112; *22*; *94*, 112; *366ff*, 27
Archilochus: *T 4 Tarditi*, 108, 113
Aristophanes: *Clouds 498*, 119; *Lysistrata 1020*, 119
Callimachus: *Aetia I fr.2 Pf*, 108
Diodorus: *4.39.1*, 98
Empedocles: *fr.96*, 111
Epimenides: *fr.1*, 36
Euripides: *Bacchae 274ff*, 58; *Heracles 20*, 30; *420*, 112; *fr.312n$^2$*, 111
Herodotus: *7.61.3*, 117
Hesiod: *Catalogue of Women*, 96, 97; *Theogony 1*, 10; *1–21*, 10; *1–35*, 11; *1–103*, 52; *1–115*, 4, 6, 8; *10*, 11; *11*, 18; *11f*, 12; *11ff*, 108; *11–21*, 12; *12*, 112; *13f*, 12; *15*, 12; *16f*, 12; *18*, 12; *19*, 12; *20*, 12; *21*, 12; *22–34*, 10; *25*, 11; *26*, 59; *28*, 115; *31*, 112; *31–34*, 108; *32*, 12; *33*, 12, 13; *33f*, 36; *35*, 10, 11, 12, 18, 37, 40, 108, 113; *36*, 10, 11, 110; *36–39*, 108; *36–52*, 10; *36–104*, 11; *38*, 12; *40*, 110; *44*, 12; *44ff*, 13, 14; *45*, 12, 13; *45f*, 12; *45ff*, 13; *45–50*, 12; *46*, 13; *46ff*, 108; *48*, 47, 12, 18, 21, 108; *48*, 108; *49*, 12, 13; *50*, 12; *53*, 110; *53–67*, 10; *54*, 39; *62*, 11; *68ff*, 11, 28; *68–76*, 10; *71ff*, 14; *71–73*, 18; *71–74*, 18; *73*, 25, 110, 111; *75*, 14, 108; *77–103*, 10; *80*, 112; *81*, 57; *82*, 112; *83f*, 92; *88*, 112; *94f*, 14; *96*, 60, 112; *98f*, 39; *101*, 14; *104*, 10, 11, 13, 14, 52; *105*, 13, 24; *105ff*, 5, 6, 14, 20; *105–7*, 108; *105–15*, 10, 26, 41; *106*, 13, 108; *106f*, 15; *106–15*, 19; *107*, 110; *108*, 108; *108–10*, 15, 108; *109*, 108; *110*, 108; *111*, 13, 15, 108; *111–13*, 108; *112*, 8, 20, 109; *112f*, 13, 15, 22; *114*, 11; *115*, 13; *116*, 15, 23; *116ff*, 12; *116–32*, 4, 108; *116–53*, 6; *116–210*, 8; *116–382*, 107; *116–885*, 23; *116–937*, 99; *117*, 23; *119*, 23; *123f*, 23; *124*, 108; *126–53*, 23; *127*, 23, 108; *132*, 18, 23; *133–53*, 5; *133–210*, 12, 15; *137*, 24; *141*, 18; *154–210*, 5, 6, 8; *157*, 33; *158*, 33, 113; *160*, 32; *162*, 37; *163ff*, 33; *164*, 110; *165*, 110; *168ff*, 33; *174*, 33, 37; *176*, 109; *178*, 33, 113; *180*, 110; *182*, 33; *185*, 16; *188*, 110; *192*, 110, 111; *197*, 7, 26, 111; *198*, 110; *200*, 110; *203*, 109; *204*, 7, 111; *207*, 110; *210*, 26; *211f*, 23; *211–32*, 5, 6, 8, 13, 15; *211–336*, 6; *211–458*, 5; *217*, 111; *225ff*, 54; *226–32*, 9; *228*, 115; *233–69*, 5; *233–336*, 6, 8, 13, 15; *262*, 110; *263ff*, 92; *270*, 107; *270–336*, 5, 20; *275*, 107; *276*, 30; *277*, 39; *279*, 94; *280*, 39; *281*, 107; *282*, 26; *285*, 98; *286*, 29; *287*, 8, 91; *287–90*, 16; *287–93*, 107; *289*, 39, 91; *293*, 39; *295*, 29, 31, 89, 91, 112; *296*, 107; *297*, 107; *298–300*, 107; *299*, 29; *301*, 107, 112; *301ff*, 35; *302*, 107; *304*, 30, 91, 107, 111; *306*, 29, 35, 39, 90, 91, 98, 110; *309*, 8, 107; *310*, 29; *311*, 8, 23; *313*, 8, 30, 91; *314*, 24; *315*, 31, 98; *316*, 39, 89, 90, 91; *317*, 32; *318*, 29, 30; *319*, 29, 89, 90, 91, 112, 122; *321*, 30; *322*, 29; *323*, 29, 30; *324*, 29; *325*, 39, 91, 107; *325f*, 92; *326*, 8, 30, 39, 89, 91, 112; *327*, 8, 30; *328*, 24, 111; *329*, 24, 30, 31, 33; *330*, 24, 30, 39; *331*, 30; *332*, 39, 91; *333*, 90, 91; *334*, 29; *335*, 107; *336*, 107; *336f*, 92; *337ff*, 5, 108; *337–82*, 6; *337–616*, 8, 12, 15; *347*, 7, 112; *361*, 23; *383–403*, 6; *383–452*,

107; *386–403*, 5, 20; *392–96*, 20, 21; *398*, 21, 110; *403*, 21, 112; *404–52*, 6; *410*, 109, 123; *412–52*, 20; *413f*, 21; *416–52*, 5, 20; *422*, 109; *423f*, 18; *424*, 109; *425*, 109; *427*, 21; *437*, 21; *443*, 21; *444*, 123; *447*, 21; *453*, 110; *453–506*, 6; *453–616*, 107; *455*, 110; *457*, 18, 21; *459*, 33; *459–500*, 5; *460*, 33, 37; *462*, 33, 112; *465*, 30; *468*, 21, 111; *469ff*, 33; *472*, 110; *472f*, 16; *474ff*, 33; *475*, 25; *476*, 25, 112; *477*, 25; *480*, 110; *482*, 33; *483*, 33; *485*, 37; *486*, 112; *487*, 33, 37; *490*, 25, 33; *491*, 112; *494*, 18, 25; *494–96*, 98; *496*, 21, 25, 32; *498ff*, 92; *500*, 37; *501ff*, 24; *502*, 98, 110; *506*, 18, 110, 111; *507–616*, 6; *513f*, 98; *514–16*, 35; *515f*, 98; *517–20*, 35; *518*, 112; *520*, 22, 112; *521ff*, 25; *521–25*, 35; *521–34*, 35; *521–616*, 5, 20; *524*, 33; *526ff*, 35, 112; *526–28*, 35; *529*, 22; *529–31*, 33, 35; *532*, 35; *533*, 35, 112; *534*, 18, 30, 35; *535*, 24, 35, 55, 98, 112; *535ff*, 35; *535–37*, 33; *538*, 25; *539*, 33, 37; *540*, 32; *542*, 21; *542ff*, 33; *543*, 25, 33, 112; *544*, 109, 112; *545*, 30, 110; *547*, 32; *550*, 30, 110; *552*, 24; *553*, 33; *555*, 32; *556*, 24; *559*, 30, 110, 112; *560*, 32; *561*, 30, 110; *564*, 24, 34; *569*, 24; *570*, 24, 34; *571*, 27, 32; *572*, 30; *574*, 33; *575*, 94; *576f*, 93; *576–84*, 33, 93; *578ff*, 93; *579*, 27, 32; *580*, 32, 110; *581*, 94; *581–84*, 94; *582*, 33, 110; *584*, 33; *585*, 94; *586*, 34; *587*, 94; *589*, 24, 25, 29; *592*, 24, 33; *594*, 33; *595*, 33; *599*, 33, 37; *600*, 24; *602*, 113; *606*, 109; *608*, 98, 109; *614–16*, 35; *615f*, 112; *616*, *35*, *112*; *617*, 110; *617ff*, 23; *617–728*, 5; *617–735*, 6; *617–820*, 12, 15; *617–885*, 107; *629–36*, 27; *637*, 18; *643*, 21, 111; *650*, 30; *653*, 30, 112; *661*, 30, 111; *674*, 30; *675*, 37; *681*, 111; *682*, 27;

*689*, 21; *702ff*, 27; *705*, 18; *710*, 18, 21; *721–819*, 8; *727*, 110; *729–819*, 5; *730*, 30, 110; *736ff*, 22; *736–819*, 6, 20, 22; *745ff*, 22; *746*, 112; *758ff*, 22; *767ff*, 22; *775ff*, 22; *775–806*, 7; *779*, 112; *782–93*, 9; *799*, 112; *801*, 22; *802*, 112; *803*, 111; *807ff*, 22; *811ff*, 22; *820*, 23; *820f*, 26; *820–80*, 5, 8, 15, 20; *821*, 92; *822*, 96; *825*, 29; *827*, 29; *828*, 29; *829*, 33; *832*, 30; *833*, 30; *834*, 30; *836*, 29; *837*, 27, 33, 112; *837f*, 27; *838*, 21, 111; *845*, 29; *849*, 111; *850*, 112; *850–52*, 26; *858*, 27, 32; *859*, 27, 112; *859–67*, 28; *860*, 28; *861*, 111; *862*, 28; *864*, 28; *865*, 28; *866*, 27, 32, 111; *868*, 39; *871*, 110; *872–80*, 29; *874*, 31, 33; *877*, 24; *879*, 24; *881*, 23; *881–85*, 15, 23; *881–929*, 8; *881–1022*, 6; *882–85*, 33; *883*, 112; *884f*, 12, 20; *885*, 15, 42, 98, 109; *886*, 41, 109, 112, 123; *886ff*, 8; *886–916*, 16; *886–926*, 5, 15; *886–964*, 107; *887*, 30, 112; *889*, 30; *890*, 30, 33, 37; *892*, 33, 112; *892f*, 27; *894*, 27, 30; *896*, 30, 110, 111; *897*, 16, 17, 112; *897f*, 98; *899*, 33, 37; *900*, 96, 97; *900–63*, 97; *901*, 97; *901–64*, 19; *901–1020*, 97; *904*, 30; *904–6*, 111; *912*, 123; *912–14*, 16; *914*, 17; *915*, 39; *921*, 109; *923*, 112; *924–29*, 33, 109; *927*, 18; *927–29*, 17; *927–37*, 5; *927–62*, 15; *927–1020*, 15; *928*, 109; *929*, 32, 96, 112; *930*, 99; *930ff*, 99; *931ff*, 99; *931–33a*, 109; *932*, 110, 111; *933*, 99; *933–62*, 17; *937*, 16, 96, 109; *938*, 99, 123; *938f*, 109; *938–62*, 5; *938–64*, 123; *939*, 96, 99; *939ff*, 99; *940ff*, 107; *942*, 39; *946*, 109; *948*, 99, 109; *949*, 39; *950–55*, 97; *953*, 109; *954f*, 39; *955*, 96; *956–62*, 16; *957*, 112; *960*, 111; *961f*, 16; *962*, 96; *963*, 96; *963–68*, 5, 15, 123; *964*, 15, 96; *965*, 16, 40, 123; *965ff*, 97; *965–68*, 15; *965–*

*91*, 123; *969*, 123; *969ff*, 15; *969–74*, 16; *969–1020*, 5, 15; *970*, 98; *975*, 123; *975–78*, 16; *979ff*, 89; *979–83*, 16; *980*, 123; *984–91*, 16; *985*, 112; *986ff*, 15; *992*, 112; *992–1002*, 16; *992–1018*, 123; *995*, 112; *1001*, 110; *1003*, 16; *1005*, 123; *1009*, 98; *1016*, 112; *1018*, 98; *1019–22*, 96; *1020*, 97; *1021f*, 5, 15; *Works and Days*; *1*, 69, 102; *1–10*, 47; *1–382*, 113; *3*, 74; *4*, 22, 74; *5*, 74; *5–9*, 56; *6*, 61, 74, 103, 117; *6f*, 21; *7*, 74; *9*, 64, 116; *9f*, 52; *10*, 49, 52, 64, 74, 115, 116, 117; *11*, 52, 54, 118; *11–26*, 47, 86, 115; *13*, 100; *14*, 56, 101, 105, 116; *15*, 54, 102, 116; *15f*, 56, 57; *16*, 56, 57; *16–26*, 115; *18*, 56; *19*, 101, 114; *20*, 54; *20–26*, 57; *21*, 54, 58; *22*, 58; *22f*, 61, 117; *23*, 117; *25f*, 59; *26*, 50, 102, 117; *27*, 52, 64, 74, 83, 101, 103, 118, 120; *27ff*, 65; *27–41*, 47, 115; *28*, 54, 117; *29*, 70, 83, 117; *31*, 70; *31f*, 61; *32*, 61, 104, 117; *33*, 60, 105, 116; *34*, 61, 117, 119; *35*, 103; *36*, 114, 116; *36ff*, 118; *36–40*, 119; *38*, 61; *39*, 116, 117, 118; *40*, 49, 53, 105, 117; *41*, 83, 103, 115; *42*, 49, 62, 115, 117; *42–105*, 47; *43*, 54; *43f*, 84; *45*, 51, 105, 114; *45f*, 65, 115; *46*, 54, 102; *47*, 75, 100; *47f*, 53; *48*, 120; *49*, 104, 114; *50*, 49; *51*, 101; *56*, 122; *57*, 117; *59*, 117; *62*, 117; *63*, 72; *64*, 54; *65*, 72; *67*, 75, 84, 104, 105; *68–101*, 105; *71*, 72, 81; *72–76*, 94; *73*, 117; *74f*, 93; *75*, 93; *77*, 101; *78*, 75, 104, 105, 120, 121; *79*, 56; *80*, 72, 117; *81*, 100; *82*, 62, 117, 122; *83*, 100; *85*, 117; *85f*, 83, 116; *86*, 117; *91*, 100, 115; *94*, 72; *95*, 49, 104, 114; *96*, 72; *96f*, 72; *99*, 56; *101*, 119; *103*, 62; *105*, 104; *106*, 66; *106–201*, 47; *107*, 83, 100; *108*, 55, 100, 116, 117; *109*, 100; *110*, 100; *111*, 55, 111, 116; *112*, 100, 105, 117; *113*, 100, 104; *115*, 63; *117*, 53, 63, 101; *117f*, 53; *119*, 54, 63, 103, 115; *120*, 57, 117; *121*, 100, 106; *122*, 56, 69; *123*, 62, 100; *123–5*, 106; *124*, 54, 102, 116; *124f*, 62; *125*, 63, 102; *126*, 117; *128*, 100; *131*, 58, 117; *133*, 100; *134*, 116; *135*, 62; *135f*, 57; *138*, 55, 57, 101; *139*, 100, 117; *140*, 100, 106; *141*, 69; *142*, 57, 100; *143*, 100, 116; *146*, 54, 116; *148*, 116; *150*, 58; *151*, 54, 69, 116; *154*, 69; *156*, 100, 106; *156–73*, 49; *157*, 100; *158*, 50, 101; *159*, 69; *160*, 100; *161*, 101, 116; *164*, 68; *165*, 68; *168*, 101; *170*, 100, 105; *172f*, 53; *173*, 63, 101; *173c*, 57; *174–76*, 62; *177*, 104; *178*, 117; *179*, 100; *180*, 100; *182*, 63; *184*, 57, 69; *186*, 69, 101; *187*, 54, 57, 62, 69, 102; *189*, 84; *190*, 116; *191*, 116; *192*, 116; *193*, 61; *195*, 104, 117; *200*, 62, 69; *202*, 64; *202–12*, 47; *202–85*, 115; *203*, 86; *204*, 86; *207*, 114; *208*, 86, 102, 114; *209*, 100; *210*, 63; *213*, 61, 63, 74, 103, 116, 118; *213–47*, 62, 118; *213–382*, 47; *214*, 63, 116; *217*, 63, 116; *218*, 62, 117; *219*, 56, 105, 116; *220*, 116; *221*, 105, 116, 117, 118; *222*, 58, 84; *223*, 62, 63, 102; *223f*, 63; *224*, 103; *225*, 116; *226*, 116; *227*, 58, 84; *229*, 56, 105, 116; *230*, 58; *231*, 54, 63, 103; *232*, 62, 116; *232–34*, 53; *235*, 63; *236*, 115; *237*, 53, 63, 101; *238*, 54, 102, 116; *239*, 56, 105, 116; *240*, 58, 61, 84; *242*, 56, 62; *243*, 58; *244*, 58, 103; *245*, 56; *247*, 56, 102, 115; *248*, 64; *248f*, 61; *248–73*, 62, 118; *248–92*, 53; *249*, 116; *250*, 105, 116; *251*, 62, 117; *252*, 100; *253*, 62, 100; *253–5*, 106; *254*, 54, 102, 116; *254f*, 62; *255*, 102; *256*, 62, 116; *257*, 100, 117; *260*, 56, 104; *262*, 105, 115, 116; *263f*, 118; *264*, 48, 105, 116, 117; *266*, 56, 117; *267*, 56, 83, 103;

*268,* 100; *269,* 58, 84, 116; *270,*
62, 116; *271,* 116; *272,* 116; *273,*
64; *274,* 64, 74, 83, 100, 103, 104,
118, 120; *275,* 61, 63, 116; *275ff,*
114; *276,* 56, 63, 117; *276ff,* 50;
*276–80,* 62; *278,* 116; *279,* 114,
116; *280,* 116; *281,* 56; *283,* 104,
116; *286,* 53, 54, 58, 60, 61, 74,
83, 86, 105, 117, 119, 120; *286–
326,* 61; *287ff,* 86; *288,* 103; *288f,*
61; *289,* 117; *289f,* 61; *291,* 100;
*293,* 83, 103; *295,* 56, 83; *297,* 83,
100; *298–316,* 53; *299,* 58, 60, 74,
118, 120; *300,* 57, 61, 117; *301,*
105, 119; *302,* 58; *303,* 85, 106,
117; *304–6,* 61; *305,* 104; *306,* 54,
57, 74; *307,* 61, 105, 119; *308,* 54;
*309,* 54, 57; *311,* 54; *312,* 54, 61,
74, 117; *314,* 54; *315,* 61, 102,
117; *316,* 48, 54, 74, 83, 102, 116;
*316–19,* 61; *317,* 58, 103; *320,* 61,
74, 101, 114; *320–41,* 120; *321,*
116; *323,* 104, 120; *325,* 58, 61,
103, 107, 117; *325f,* 61; *326,* 74,
100; *327,* 74; *332,* 101; *334,* 54;
*335,* 74, 102, 120; *335–80,* 73;
*336,* 74, 85, 106, 117; *336–41,* 76;
*337,* 120; *338f,* 76; *340,* 75, 100;
*341,* 74; *342,* 57, 74; *342–48,* 76;
*342–82,* 120; *343,* 103, 106; *345,*
56, 75; *346,* 103, 122; *349,* 59;
*349–78,* 76; *350f,* 74; *351,* 58;
*353,* 57; *354ff,* 59; *354–58,* 117;
*360,* 57, 60; *361f,* 74; *363,* 58;
*364,* 101; *364f,* 58; *367,* 58, 74,
105; *368,* 84, 103; *370,* 57; *370–
72,* 120; *371,* 75, 121; *371–75,* 82;
*373,* 74, 75, 104, 120; *373f,* 84;
*374,* 74, 75, 119, 120; *375,* 75,
120; *376,* 58, 75; *378,* 120; *380,*
48, 74; *381,* 100; *381f,* 74; *382,*
54, 103, 113, 118; *383,* 54, 56;
*383ff,* 115; *383–492,* 70; *384,* 71;
*385,* 100, 119; *386,* 119; *387,* 100,
119; *388,* 59, 119; *389,* 103; *391f,*
71, 119; *393,* 54, 56, 117; *394,* 58;
*394ff,* 49; *395,* 50, 58; *396,* 56;
*397,* 54, 61, 74, 117, 118; *397ff,*

120; *398,* 54, 65, 105, 117; *399,*
118; *400,* 70; *401, 119; *402,* 59,
70; *403,* 59, 83, 117; *403f,* 70,
105; *404, 58, 83, 116; *405,* 58, 71,
121; *405f,* 59, 71, 82; *406,* 121;
*407,* 58, 101; *409,* 54; *410,* 56;
*411,* 70, 105; *412,* 54; *414,* 71;
*414–19,* 121; *414–36,* 49; *416,* 56;
*417,* 56; *422,* 54; *423ff,* 71; *423–
26,* 51; *423–36,* 51; *424,* 51; *427–
36,* 51; *428,* 58, 101; *429,* 115,
116; *430,* 56, 71; *432,* 58; *434,* 51;
*438,* 54; *439,* 56; *440,* 51, 54; *443,*
54; *444,* 54, 101; *444f,* 56; *447,*
101; *448,* 49, 56, 71, 83, 116; *449,*
86; *450ff,* 71; *452,* 100; *453,* 115;
*453f,* 59; *454,* 54; *455,* 115; *456,*
117; *458f,* 56; *461,* 101; *462,* 49,
71; *463,* 101; *464,* 56; *465,* 57;
*466,* 56, 104; *467,* 100; *469–71,*
56; *471,* 114; *474,* 57; *476,* 100;
*479,* 65, 71, 103; *483,* 100, 104;
*483f,* 60, 69; *486,* 71, 83; *487,*
100; *488,* 56; *491,* 100; *493,* 70,
71, 82, 119, 120; *493ff,* 70; *493–
563,* 70; *494,* 54; *495,* 58, 82; *498,*
70, 72; *499,* 70; *500,* 58, 70, 72,
103; *501,* 70, 105; *502,* 56, 121;
*503,* 70; *504,* 71, 119; *506,* 56;
*506ff,* 82; *507,* 72, 102; *508,* 119;
*510,* 100; *513,* 100; *515,* 119; *517,*
101; *518,* 56, 71; *519,* 101; *519f,*
71; *519–21,* 82; *520,* 72; *521,* 56,
72; *523,* 58, 72, 101; *524,* 72; *525,*
58, 70; *526,* 71, 117; *527,* 58, 71;
*528,* 73; *530,* 102; *531,* 100; *533,*
71, 72, 73; *536,* 83, 102, 116;
*536ff,* 71; *539,* 102; *541,* 119; *543,*
104; *544,* 119; *547,* 56; *549,* 101,
102; *553,* 56; *554,* 54, 101; *559,*
82; *562,* 71, 100; *564,* 65, 71, 103;
*564ff,* 49; *564–617,* 70; *566,* 56,
119; *568,* 71, 83; *570,* 101; *572,*
56, 119; *573,* 119, 121; *575ff,* 71;
*577,* 105; *578,* 54; *579,* 54; *582–
96,* 49; *583,* 65, 86, 102, 114; *584,*
66, 104; *585,* 114; *586,* 62; *587,*
56, 82; *588,* 75; *592,* 104; *593,* 82;

*594*, 56, 82; *597*, 56, 58, 104, 121;
*597f*, 121; *598*, 56, 101; *599*, 85,
106; *600*, 100; *601*, 58, 101, 118;
*602f*, 121; *602ff*, 71; *604*, 84, 104;
*604f*, 84; *607*, 102; *608*, 57; *609f*,
56; *610*, 119; *611*, 74, 103, 118;
*612*, 71; *614*, 56, 58, 100, 117;
*615*, 56, 101, 119; *615f*, 71; *616f*,
105; *617*, 48; *618*, 67; *618ff*, 50;
*618–29*, 67; *618–30*, 67; *618–45*,
67; *618–94*, 47; *619*, 56, 101;
*619ff*, 67; *622*, 66; *623*, 54, 83,
102, 116; *623f*, 68; *627*, 58, 101;
*629*, 51, 105; *630*, 67; *630–40*, 67;
*631*, 67; *631–40*, 67; *631–62*, 67;
*633*, 61, 74, 83, 105, 117; *634*, 58,
68; *638*, 57; *639*, 104; *639f*, 68;
*641*, 54, 74, 103, 118; *641f*, 105;
*641–45*, 67; *641–47*, 67; *643*, 67;
*644*, 67; *645f*, 67; *646*, 102; *646–
62*, 50, 67; *647*, 58; *648*, 68; *648–
62*, 67; *650*, 72, 102; *650ff*, 66;
*650–59*, 119; *651–59*, 68; *652*, 68,
72, 119; *653*, 68, 73; *654–59*, 113;
*655*, 120; *655–59*, 52; *657*, 68, 72,
73; *658*, 57, 69; *659*, 50, 65, 69,
102; *660*, 68; *661*, 60, 68, 69, 83,
104; *661f*, 69; *662*, 57, 102; *663*,
65, 78, 103; *663ff*, 67; *663–77*, 67;
*663–94*, 67; *664*, 66, 104; *665*, 68;
*666*, 51; *672*, 67; *673*, 58, 101;
*674*, 119; *675*, 58; *678ff*, 114;
*678–86*, 67; *678–88*, 67; *679*, 100;
*684*, 100; *685*, 104; *687*, 83; *687f*,
68, 105; *688*, 48, 68, 100, 116;
*689*, 118; *689–94*, 67; *690*, 67;
*693*, 51; *693f*, 51; *694*, 65, 74,
114; *695*, 58, 82; *695ff*, 118; *695–
701*, 82; *695–714*, 76; *695–764*,
47, 73, 74; *696*, 100; *697*, 100;
*699*, 75, 121; *700*, 75, 103, 106;
*702*, 120; *704*, 75, 82; *705*, 75, 82;
*706*, 69, 75, 118; *707*, 69, 82, 104;
*707–13*, 75; *708*, 56; *709*, 104;
*712*, 56, 57, 116; *713*, 57; *714*,
104; *715*, 76; *719*, 114; *720*, 101;
*722f*, 76; *723*, 101; *724*, 76; *724f*,
76; *724–59*, 120; *727*, 76; *728*,

100; *730*, 76; *733*, 58, 101; *741*,
85, 106, 117; *742*, 117; *742f*, 76;
*742–45*, 76; *754*, 100; *756*, 117;
*760*, 103; *760–64*, 78, 120; *762*,
74; *764*, 48, 117; *765*, 57, 79, 81;
*765–828*, 47, 78, 79; *766*, 84, 114,
121; *767*, 54, 83; *768*, 83; *769*, 57,
79, 81, 101, 104; *769–79*, 78; *770*,
80, 101, 121; *770–72a*, 79; *771*,
57; *772*, 120; *772–79*, 80; *772a*,
79; *772b–74*, 79; *773*, 54; *775*, 84;
*779*, 54; *780f*, 80; *780–97*, 80, 81,
82; *781*, 114; *783*, 80, 82; *784*, 80,
82; *785*, 80, 82; *786*, 104; *788*, 57,
80, 82, 101; *789*, 104, 120, 121;
*790*, 79; *792–95*, 81; *793*, 80, 104;
*794*, 79, 80, 82, 101; *796*, 84, 104;
*797*, 79, 80; *798–801*, 80; *800*, 58,
82; *801*, 81; *802–4*, 80; *804*, 57;
*805*, 104, 121; *805–8*, 80; *806*, 85,
106; *808*, 81; *809*, 80, 81; *810*, 81;
*810–13*, 80, 84; *810–21*, 78; *812*,
80, 82, 121; *814*, 78, 114; *814–18*,
80; *815*, 81, 83, 84, 103; *816*, 84,
102; *817*, 84, 102; *817f*, 81; *819*,
80, 81, 82, 83, 84, 101; *819–20*,
81; *819–21*, 80, 121; *820*, 114,
121; *821*, 81, 84, 89; *822*, 78, 81,
83, 103, 104; *824*, 100; *826f*, 83;
*827*, 54; *828*, 81, 83; fr.2–3 MW,
112
Homer: *Iliad*, 47; *1.239*, 117; *1.400*, 17;
*1.593*, 27; *8.402ff*, 111; *8.478*,
112; *14.322*, 99; *15.187ff*, 20;
*15.189f*, 109; *18.117ff*, 97; *23.87*,
119; *Kypria fr.5*, 94; *Odyssey, 9.108f*,
117; *11.432*, 30; *11.601ff*, 98;
*14.58*, 60; *14.193ff*, 65, 68;
*17.382–85*, 117; *18*, 48, 59, 117;
*18.327*, 119
Homeric Hymns: *Aphrodite (V) 4f*, 94;
*293*, 10; *Aphrodite (VI) 3f*, 108; *7*,
93, 94; *18*, 93; *19f*, 10; *21*, 10;
*Apollo (III) 300*, 90; *307ff*, 18, 27;
*319*, 111; *546*, 10; *Demeter (II)*, 10;
*495*, 10; *Dionysus (VII) 41*, 94;
*Hermes (IV) 580*, 10; *IX.9*, 10; *X.4f*,
10; *6*, 10; *XI.5*, 10; *XV.4*, 108;

*9*, 10; *XVIII.11*, 10; *XIX.49*, 10;
*XX.2*, 108; *8*, 10; *XXII*, 10; *XXIV.5*,
10; *XXV.7*, 10; *XXVI*, 10; *11f*, 10;
*XXVII.22*, 10; *XXVIII*, 10; *18*, 10;
*XXIX.14*, 10; *XXX.19*, 10;
*XXXIII.19*, 10
Pausanias: *1.3.1*, 15
Pherecydes: *3 F 7*, 89

Pindar: *Isthmian 8*, 109
Plato: *Phaedrus*, 113; *Republic 372c*, 116;
     *474a*, 119; *Statesman 272a5*, 115
Semonides: *fr.7 W*, 94
Sophocles: *Trachiniae 144–47*, 120;
     *1011f*, 30
Stesichorus: *fr.239 PMG*, 18
*Tale of Ullikummi*, 23, 110

# INDEX OF SCHOLARS

Aly, W., 74, 108, 110, 113, 114
Arthur, M. B., 108, 111
Athanassakis, A. N., 114, 116
Barron, J. P., 4, 74, 110, 115
Benardete, S., 74, 113, 114, 116, 117, 119, 120, 121
Beye, C. R., 114, 116
Blech, M., 122
Blusch, J., 48, 74, 113, 114, 115, 117
Boedeker, D., 110
Bona Quaglia, L., 74, 86, 113, 114, 115, 116, 117, 118, 119, 120, 122
Bradley, E. M., 96, 107, 108, 110, 113
Brommer, F., 123
Brown, N. O., 5, 6, 96, 97, 107, 109, 110, 113
Clay, J. S., 110
Combellack, F., 107
Daly, L. W., 114, 118
Delgado, J. A. F., 114, 116, 120
Derossi, G., 110
Detienne, M., 116, 118, 120
Dickie, M. W., 114
Diller, H., 74, 114, 116, 117, 120, 122
Dornseiff, F., 114
Edwards, G. P., 51, 77, 119
Fontenrose, J., 115, 116
Frankel, H., 114, 117
Friedländer, P., 93, 107, 108, 110, 111, 113, 114, 115, 117
Fritz, K. von, 108, 114, 118
Fuss, W., 74, 113, 114, 115, 116, 118
Goettling, C., 93, 113
Griffin, J., 4, 68, 116, 118
Griffith, M., 21, 68, 108, 110, 118
Groningen, B. A. van, 74, 96, 108, 109, 114, 115, 116, 120
Guthrie, W. K. C., 111
Harder, R., 115
Heath, M., 61, 74, 78, 113, 114, 116, 120, 122
Heckenbach, J., 110
Janko, R., 107, 108

Jensen, M. S., 113, 114, 117, 118, 120, 122
Jiménez, A. P., 78, 120, 122
Jones, N. F., 114, 117, 118
Kambylis, A., 112, 113
Kerschensteiner, J., 74, 113, 114, 116, 117, 120
Kirk, G. S., 4, 96, 107, 109, 110, 116, 120
Krafft, F., 85, 122
Kraus, T., 110
Krug, A., 123
Kumaniecki, K., 114, 116, 118, 120
Lemke, D., 89, 90, 91
Lendle, O., 94, 110, 122
Lesky, A., 109
Liebermann, W., 115
Livrea, E., 115
Maehler, H., 108, 113
Marg, W., 93, 96, 109, 110, 122, 123
Marquandt, P. A., 108, 112
Mathiessen, K., 114, 116, 118
Mazon, P., 93, 108, 109, 110, 112, 113, 114, 118, 120, 122
McEvilley, T., 122
Minton, W. W., 107, 108
Mondi, R., 4, 109, 110, 111, 112
Munding, H., 48, 114, 117
Nagy, G., 48, 96, 108, 113, 114, 117, 118
Neitzel, H., 108, 110, 111, 122
Nicolai, W., 48, 50, 67, 70, 74, 114, 115, 116, 118, 119, 120, 121, 122
Northrup, M. D., 113, 123
Nussbaum, G., 119
Østerud, S., 114
Page, D. L., 123
Paley, F. A., 93
Peabody, B., 48, 59, 114, 117, 119
Pfister, F., 110
Philippson, P., 110, 113
Philips, F. C. Jr., 110, 112
Pickard-Cambridge, A. W., 122
Prellwitz, W., 110
Puelma, M., 119

Renehan, R., 114, 117, 120
Richardson, N. J., 114, 119, 120, 122
Robert, C., 93, 107, 110, 112, 122
Rodgers, V. A., 114
Römisch, E., 115
Roesch, P., 78, 120, 121
Rosenmeyer, T. J., 114
Rowe, C. J., 116
Rudhardt, M., 109
Rzach, A., 93
Said, S., 107, 110, 111
Samuel, A. E., 79
Schmid, W., 4, 74, 96, 107, 109, 110, 113, 114, 119
Schmidt, J.-U., 48, 74, 115, 116, 117, 118
Schoemann, G. F., 109, 123
Schwabl, H., 74, 90, 91, 93, 96, 97, 99, 107, 108, 109, 110, 111, 113, 114, 118, 119, 120, 122, 123
Schwenn, F., 108, 109, 110, 111, 112, 122
Scodel, R., 119
Sellschopp, I., 93, 94, 111, 114, 120, 121, 122
Siegmann, E., 90, 91, 108, 122
Slater, W. J., 113
Slatkin, L. M., 109
Smith, C. H., 95, 123
Smith, P., 114, 118, 122

Solmsen, F., 4, 16, 25, 62, 74, 79, 93, 96, 108, 109, 110, 111, 112, 114, 116, 118, 119, 121, 122
Steitz, A., 58, 74, 113, 118, 119
Susemihl, F., 113, 115
Svenbro, J., 59, 113
Teggart, F. J., 113, 116
Thalmann, W. G., 8, 9, 74, 89, 108, 109, 110, 112, 114, 118, 119, 120
Usener, H., 109
Verdenius, W. J., 48, 53, 74, 79, 108, 109, 111, 112, 113, 114, 118, 120, 121, 122
Vernant, J. P., 55, 109, 110, 111, 112, 116
Vos, H., 107
Walcot, P., 4, 5, 6, 8, 9, 38, 48, 96, 107, 110, 111, 112, 113, 114, 116, 119, 120, 122
Webster, T. B. L., 123
West, M. L., 4, 5, 7, 8, 15, 17, 23, 25, 28, 36, 37, 47, 48, 50, 51, 57, 60, 62, 65, 67, 70, 73, 74, 77, 79, 89, 90, 91, 93, 96, 97, 98, 99, 107, 108, 109, 110, 111, 112, 113, 114, 115, 116, 117, 118, 119, 120, 121, 122, 123
Wilamowitz-Moellendorff, U. von, 74
Wolf, F. A., 93
Ziegler, K., 108, 123